Breaking down barriers

DATE DUE

Demco, Inc. 38-293

Breaking down barriers

Certificate in Workplace Language, Literacy and Numeracy Training

Edited by

Chris Holland, Fiona Frank, and Jaine Chisholm Caunt

Published by the National Institute of Adult
Continuing Education (England & Wales)
21 De Montfort Street, Leicester LE1 7GE

Company registration number 2603322 Charity registration number 1002775

First edition published 1998

Second edition, revised by Chris Holland and
Jaine Chisholm Caunt

Additional contributions to the second edition by
Sandra Pegum and Alexander Braddell

Contributors to the first edition
Chris Holland, Fiona Frank, Sue Jeffery, Alison Marquand,
Alison Noel

© NIACE 2001
Reprinted 2002,2003

Cataloguing in Publication Data

A CIP record for this title is available from the British Library

ISBN 1 86201 130 3

Typeset by Q3 Bookwork, Loughborough
Cover design by Boldface, London
Printed in Great Britain by Antony Rowe

Contents

SECTION FOUR

Foreword

At a time of great change and dynamism in UK adult basic education policy, we are proud to be producing a new edition of this course book, designed to support the Workplace Basic Skills Network *Breaking Down Barriers* (*BDB1*) Initial Certificate in Workplace Language, Literacy and Numeracy Training. At the time of writing over 600 practitioners in the UK – and some in Ireland and New Zealand – have undertaken this accredited course. In addition there is a small but growing network of qualified and experienced 'Approved Network Trainers' who have undertaken the training qualifying them to deliver the course to practitioners around the UK on behalf of the Network.

The first edition of *Breaking Down Barriers* was written by Chris Holland, Fiona Frank, Sue Jeffery, Alison Marquand and Alison Noel.

This new edition has been extensively revised by Chris Holland and Jaine Chisholm Caunt, with additional contributions from Sandra Pegum and Alexander Braddell. It includes new material on developing a holistic, integrated approach to workplace provision, and reflects the changing policy context in the UK at the beginning of the 21st century.

This book – and the course – reflects a view of workplace language, literacy and numeracy held by the Workplace Basic Skills Network and many other agencies involved in this work, in which transferable, integrated basic skills are valued and promoted within company training strategies. They are partly as a consequence of workplace change, rather than being seen as a deficit in the individual worker. To meet this aim, we advocate a 'tutor-consultant' role, where the practitioner can advise on wider literacy issues within the workplace as well as providing courses linked to workplace needs for individual workers.

BDB1 is the first in the Network's pathway of qualifications for adult language, literacy and numeracy practitioners working in or moving into workplace settings. All of these programmes, which run from Initial Certificate to Postgraduate level, are designed to link professional development in this work to research-based theory, as well as to current UK and international practice (see Appendix).

We hope you enjoy using this book. We would be very pleased to hear from you about your workplace language, literacy and numeracy provision, about your professional development needs, and any comments about the content of this book.

Chris Holland, Fiona Frank and Jaine Chisholm Caunt
Workplace Basic Skills Network, CSET, Lancaster University
July 2001

Acknowledgements

We are grateful for the financial support of the Department for Education and Skills (DfES) since October 1999 for the core activities of the Workplace Basic Skills Network. This has allowed us to develop the content of this and other continuing professional development programmes, and to consolidate our other services for Network members. We could not have got to a second edition of this book without the support of provider organisations and agencies which have commissioned deliveries of the *BDB1* course since the first edition was published in 1998. We have been guided by comments from many of the 600+ practitioners who have gone through the *BDB1* programme (see Helsby, 2000). We acknowledge the support of the 'Approved Network Trainers' group and the Workplace Basic Skills Network Steering Group. Jakes Makin and staff at OCNW have been most supportive on accreditation-related issues.

We have not forgotten the financial support given when we were producing the first edition, by NIACE, Oxfordshire County Council Basic Skills At Work, The Adult College Lancaster, Suffolk Training and Enterprise Council and Derbyshire County Council Community Education Service.

We owe a lot to Virman Man in NIACE's Publications Department for his continuing support and encouragement.

Finally we would like to acknowledge the vision of David Blunkett, who set out the Adult Basic Skills Strategy between 1999 and 2001 whilst Secretary of State for Education in the Labour Government. This has made an enormous contribution to changing the *status* of workplace language, literacy and numeracy provision – no longer a 'Cinderella Service', but a mainstream, integrated, and valued area of work.

Chris Holland, Fiona Frank and Jaine Chisholm Caunt
Workplace Basic Skills Network, CSET, Lancaster University,
July 2001

How to use this book

This book will be useful for practitioners and co-ordinators of basic skills programmes, who wish to develop workplace provision. It is also designed to support the *Breaking Down Barriers* (*BDB1*) Certificate course delivered by the Workplace Basic Skills Network, but can also be read by those not attending the programme.

BDB1 is designed for experienced and qualified language, literacy and numeracy practitioners. The accredited course can be delivered by Approved Network Trainers who are all experienced workplace basic skills training programme co-ordinators and/or practitioners with a good knowledge of the background issues involved in this area of work.

The course can be offered in a variety of ways. We recommend that it is delivered either over three consecutive days, three or more weekly sessions, or in smaller sessions over a term.

To arrange for the delivery of the accredited course by an Approved Network Trainer in your area, contact:

Workplace Basic Skills Network
CSET
Lancaster University
Lancaster
LA1 4YL
tel 01524 592679
fax 01524 844788
email wbs.net@lancaster.ac.uk
website http://www.lancaster.ac.uk/wbsnet

About accreditation

Details of the Learning Outcomes, suggested assignments, and Units and Elements are included at the end of this pack. The Certificate can be achieved by participation in the programme, and the completion of a portfolio of assignments.

OCNW has accredited this course for delivery by Approved Network Trainers and can moderate the course anywhere in the UK.

Professional development pathways and contact details
Breaking Down Barriers (*BDB1*), the Initial Certificate in Workplace Basic Skills, is the first in the professional development pathways programme coordinated by the Workplace Basic Skills Network for qualified and experienced basic skills tutors working in, or moving into, workplace settings.

Other programmes include:
- BDB2 – Advanced Certificate in Workplace Basic Skills (jointly accredited by OCNW and the Department of Continuing Education at Lancaster University)

- Postgraduate Diploma in Adult Basic Education – Workplace Module (accredited by Lancaster University)

- Approved Network Trainers programme (accredited by OCNW)

- Using the Internet in Workplace Basic Skills (accredited by the Dept of Continuing Education at Lancaster University)

General concepts of workplace language, literacy and numeracy training and organisational culture

Objectives

Course participants will be able to:

- gain an understanding of the context of workplace basic skills training, and the benefits and barriers to an employer in introducing such a programme.

- identify differences between language, literacy and numeracy programme delivery in the community and in the workplace

- discuss developments and changes in workplace organisational structure

- link key concepts in quality management and training

- identify "old"- and "new"-style workplaces

- develop a profile of an organisation

- relate organisational culture to training investment

- identify the relationship between training policies and quality initiatives

Introduction

All basic skills practitioners need to know about adult language, literacy and numeracy theory and pedagogy. Basic skills practitioners delivering in workplace settings need also to know about business priorities, and how to work effectively with business to integrate language, literacy and numeracy provision into their existing organisational development and training. In particular they need to be able to:

- understand business objectives
- recognise organisational issues impacting on language, literacy and numeracy
- analyse individual and organisational language, literacy and numeracy needs
- negotiate provision that is meaningful and effective for employers and workers
- recognise cultural issues.

Throughout this book, the term *basic skills* has frequently been replaced by 'language, literacy and numeracy', reflecting the view of the government, the Workplace Basic Skills Network, NIACE and others, that 'basic skills' is an unhelpful term for describing and promoting language, literacy and numeracy development. There is a risk that the teaching of English language in the workplace may still be overlooked by 'literacy and numeracy'. Therefore we have included the term 'language' to cover the teaching of English for speakers of other languages (ESOL).

We need also to be cautious about the language that we use to promote programmes in the workplace. Managers and workers will respond well to a discussion about "workplace communications". They may not be clear about what we mean by "literacy and numeracy" or they may associate this with **ill**iteracy. Workers seen as having language, literacy or numeracy training needs may be stigmatised or even dismissed. Some examples of positive programme names that have been used by programmes around the UK include "Upskill at Work", "Workplace Communication", "Put Yourself Forward", "Core Skills" and "Essential Skills". The integration of Key Skills with other vocational training means that the term "Key Skills" has a more acceptable workplace status than language, literacy and numeracy.

When we talk about language, literacy and numeracy "provision" we mean more than just the delivery of courses. Workplace language, literacy (oral and written communications) and numeracy provision may include:

- consultancy and development work for organisations to improve oral and written communications and numeracy
- training programmes which support workers to improve oral and written communications and numeracy at work and in the community.

The approach outlined in this book challenges providers and business to think beyond individual deficits. It recognises that with the rapidly changing language, literacy and numeracy requirements of 21st century workplaces, much of the responsibility for improving the oral and written communications of workers can be, and often is, met by employers.

1. Language, literacy and numeracy provision in the context of the workplace

The following is a description of some parameters of provision.

Curriculum

- This can include ESOL, literacy (oral and written communications skills), numeracy and computer skills.

Sites

- Provision mostly takes place in the organisation's learning centre, meeting room, or elsewhere on site. It is preferable to conduct development and training on site as this increases provider visibility and accessibility, enables the provider to better understand learners' working situations, and helps integrate language, literacy and numeracy training with the organisation's general training agenda.
- However, sometimes it is necessary with small enterprises to provide training at a place that is accessible to a number of sites.

Timing and place

- Formal training programmes are held completely or partly in work time. It may be necessary to time training at the beginning or end of a shift.
- Informal training and support can be arranged to suit the employer and individuals, and may be held at workstations.
- Organisational oral and written communications development and support can be an ongoing aspect of the total contract or can be arranged as a separate contract.

Who runs programmes?

- Programmes are usually developed and run by a local training provider. Examples include the basic skills units of further education colleges, adult community education centres, and private training organisations. Programmes may also be run by the organisation's training department, using staff who are adult language, literacy and numeracy professionals.

Funding

- Under current UK policy, all language, literacy and numeracy training tuition is free. This does not include the consultancy time necessary for setting up the programme, and maintaining non-teaching contact.
- Local Learning and Skills Councils (LLSCs) can fund traditional post-16 learning in their area. They can also respond to local vocational skills needs by funding particular initiatives.
- The Union Learning Fund (ULF) can support workplace learning initiatives.
- The employer can sometimes pay for language, literacy and numeracy programmes, especially where it is seen as integral to its general training agenda.
- Provision is usually contracted through a combination of the above.

The students

- Students are often those who have been traditionally marginalised in the labour market and for whom equal opportunity considerations apply, such as women, ethnic minorities. They may also include older workers who may have to adjust to new conditions of work.
- The learners include unskilled, semi-skilled, or skilled workers, often in low-paid jobs, with little previous access

to training courses or promotion at work. They can include supervisors, who may feel they need help to cope with the increased paperwork demands of the job. In some instances they may include people with English as a second language brought in to positions of responsibility.

The organisations

- Client organisations come in all shapes and sizes. They may be public or private, manufacturing, service or agricultural, paid or voluntary employment. Organisations may be large (250+), medium (50-250) small (11-49) or 'micro' (for example, self-employed). Some organisations may have their headquarters in another country, which influences decisions on training. Others may not have a training department or budget at all.
- Organisations who have introduced new technology or systems, or have undergone structural changes, often require training to meet their new needs.

2.   A whole-organisational approach to workplace language, literacy and numeracy provision

Many organisations, used to engaging outside training consultants, understand that they are making an investment in improving quality and competitiveness, and are well prepared to pay for professional and expert services. Management consultants, for example, will spend many hours working with employers and workers (and, where appropriate, unions) at all levels to gain insight into the issues and needs of an organisation. Much of this time is spent asking questions rather than prescribing solutions, and working to gain the confidence of key personnel in the organisation. Solutions take into account the present and future directions of the whole organisation and are often jointly conceived and actioned. All consultancy time, of course, is charged to the organisation, though special development grants and national initiatives can sometimes cover these costs.

Such an approach can be adapted in order to meet fully the needs of employers and workers, and can more closely tie our work into changing organisational requirements and vocational training activities. It can lead employers and workers to place greater value on the training we offer. Too often language, literacy and numeracy providers go in to organisations apologising for, or minimising, set up and provision costs. Providers also may place the full responsibility for poor workplace literacy and numeracy practices at the feet of workers.

Workplace language, literacy and numeracy practitioners need to be able to think beyond individual deficits, and to see how provision, both in terms of organisational communications development and in terms of training, fits into the whole organisation's development and training objectives.

Workers as learners

It is helpful for practitioners to compare the circumstances under which learners in community settings and workers engage in language, literacy and numeracy training. This will enable consideration of the implications for learners at work: the advantages and disadvantages of site-based programmes, and the different ways in which workers might be vulnerable as learners in their places of employment. The table on pages 10 and 11 describes some differences between community-based and workplace-based student groups.

Promoting provision to employers

How workplaces are targeted for the promotion of language, literacy and numeracy provision, and how it is marketed and negotiated, are crucial to whether it will be successfully established. There is a range of considerations to be taken into account. A hurried, unplanned approach is counterproductive. While provision usually includes formal programmes of learning, providers can offer a range of options to employers, based on their expertise, which will improve organisation-wide communications.

The first step for practitioners is to know how language, literacy and numeracy are used in organisations, and about related issues for organisations. There is a number of factors that can present barriers to workers fulfilling the language, literacy and numeracy requirements within their workplace. These may include increased oral and written communications requirements through changed work responsibilities and roles, changed relationships and team expectations, unclear or new recording/measuring processes and documentation, and increased vocational training. Understanding these factors will help the practitioner to develop marketing material which will 'make sense to business' and make a difference to workers' literacies at work and in the community.

Differences between community-based and workplace-based student groups

Community ABE groups	Workplace ABE groups
Can be unemployed	Always employed
Come from a wide group, defined as people within the 'travel-to-learn' area of the class.	Come from a narrowly defined group of people who, at the minimum, all work for the same organisation, and often in the same department.
May not know each other at the start of the course.	May know each other quite well at the start of the course.
Have all come together for the purpose of attending the class: i.e. have made that leap of realising that they are going to be 'basic education students' among other definitions of themselves.	May well already have very firm identity at work. May have a supervisory role. May be highly skilled and experienced. May have informal mentor role. May be an 'elder' in cultural group.
Most classes are of mixed gender.	One gender may predominate depending on the group and type of work.
Other people who may have expectations for them include the practitioners, their family, friends, the accrediting bodies.	Other people who may have expectations for them, in addition to practitioners, their family, friends, accrediting body, may include their colleagues, supervisor, line leader, training manager, board of directors.
There is no requirement to declare participation in a programme. Attendance is less likely to inconvenience others.	Participation is very visible. This may affect the way in which they are viewed by people in authority. Co-workers have to provide cover during the programme.
Students are often taught in a particular subject group, for example ESOL, numeracy, by a subject specialist teacher.	Most programmes are likely to integrate aspects of language, literacy, and numeracy within a session, and are likely to be delivered by the same tutor.

Community ABE groups	Workplace ABE groups
Curriculum is based on National Core Curricula in Adult Literacy and Numeracy.	Curriculum is negotiated between practitioners and learners, taking into account accrediting bodies, supervisors, training officers and any outside funders, who may also be involved in curriculum planning and course design. Workplace qualifications may be linked to core curricula or other vocational training.
Timing is arranged for mutual convenience, at a college or other training provider's community site.	Timing is arranged for convenience of employers: this may be a difficult time for practitioners, and may also be at the end of a shift for workers.
Curriculum may include learning support for other courses the learners are following and use material from learners' outside interests.	Curriculum likely to include learning support for other courses (for example, NVQs) and use materials and examples taken from the learners' workplace.
Learners are in control of their attendance on the programme and can decide whether to attend or not each week. Of course, outside factors beyond their control (for example, illness, transport problems) may affect this.	Learners are not always in control of their own attendance on the programme: if the course is in work time, their supervisors may want to refuse permission for them to attend the course. Conversely, a supervisor or manager might require that workers attend a programme even if the workers do not consider this necessary.
Learner has free choice over time taken to progress in chosen course of study.	In some cases, a learner may be required by the employer to improve rapidly in a specific area.

Reasons for introducing provision include:

- new paperwork demands on workers at all levels
- the introduction of new technology and ICT
- new ways of working (quality circles, continuous improvement teams)
- metrication
- new quality standards and greater demands for accuracy
- new Health and Safety and Hygiene regulations
- the introduction of new qualifications
- need to retain existing staff or attract new staff
- new government initiatives to drive up language, literacy and numeracy standards.

Many companies are aware that it is more cost-effective to boost the training of existing workers than to recruit new staff.

Employers' perceptions of the benefits of workplace language, literacy and numeracy provision include:[1]

- cuts down errors
- cuts down on time taken to write reports
- facilitates the introduction of change within a organisation
- improves communication
- increases morale among workforce
- leads to more take-up of, and better participation in, work-related training courses
- leads to a better understanding of documentation and notices
- leads to more workers being able to access promotion opportunities
- increases participation in meetings
- increases number of suggestions made by workforce
- leads to a general increase in confidence
- can provide evidence towards meeting Investor in People (IiP) standards or other quality awards

[1] Frank & Hamilton (1993)

- improves employer's status within the local community
- leads to a wider participation in community life: students can help children with homework, write letters, understand bills, become more involved in leisure activities, take up non-work-related training, apply for other jobs.

Equally, there is a number of barriers perceived by employers to undertaking a programme in language, literacy or numeracy, or to engaging consultancy in organisation-wide oral and written communications development.

Some perceived barriers and difficulties in engaging in workplace language, literacy and numeracy provision, are:

- cost and time of such training
- too many orders (economic success may mean no perceived need for training)
- unwillingness to provide training for workers who may then leave
- a feeling that people ought to have learned language, literacy and numeracy in school, and that it is not the organisation's responsibility
- lack of perceived need for such training within the organisation
- a feeling that students might not come forward for the training
- lack of training space
- lack of opportunities for progression within the organisation
- difficulty of monitoring its direct benefit
- worried about an outside provider having access to the organisation's secrets or internal politics
- a failure to appreciate the connection between basic skills components and work tasks. (*ibid*)

When marketing to organisations, it is essential to locate potential 'customers' in your area, and to conduct research into their current and planned business developments. An awareness of the perceived benefits and barriers to organisations will help you to develop a marketing strategy. Although it is important to work with small as well as large enterprises, you might prefer to begin by targeting large organisations where training strategies and budgets are more likely to be in place.

If you are able to secure an initial interview/discussion with a link person in a targeted organisation, we suggest that this meeting might be used to ask questions about goals and issues arising from your research into the organisation.

Answers will inform a presentation to key management personnel. Any questions you ask of a link person, or during a presentation, should also guide managers in their thinking about how the organisation's changing systems and business developments raise specific language, literacy and numeracy issues.

Linking language, literacy and numeracy to changing workplaces

Employers appreciate the understanding that providers show of an enterprise's operations. For instance, when providers are able to make links between the need for higher literacy and numeracy competencies and the increasingly complex documentation of processes and systems required by awarding bodies, legislation and technology, this demonstrates a clear understanding of the issues facing management and workers. Unions should be able to assist you in gaining understanding and insights about workplace change.

However, it is not sufficient to speak in broad terms about workplace change. An understanding of issues for the particular sector (for example, private manufacturing) and for the individual enterprise (for example, a car assembly plant becoming increasingly automated) will build credibility and trust.

We need to be clear that workplace literacy and numeracy development is as much about work*place* communications systems as is about work*force* training. As literacy and numeracy specialists and consultants, we need to be asking about:

- how literacy and numeracy are used throughout the organisation
- what issues have appeared with their systems of communication
- how they have tried to address issues
- what the consequences have been
- how the organisation thinks you can help[2]

Integrating language, literacy and numeracy competencies with vocational competencies

Adult learning theory tells us that adults learn better when the content is contextualised. Research in other countries has shown that successful literacy and numeracy programmes integrate literacy competencies not only with workplace change, but also with vocational training. Programmes are also more successful when they are part of union learning initiatives.

Private training providers are increasingly working with the business community as they provide support in the delivery and accreditation of NVQs. Language, literacy and numeracy work may often involve providing individual support with NVQ portfolio requirements, as well as delivering accredited language, literacy and numeracy courses.

Programmes may also be linked to planned wider developments in the organisation such as:

- mergers or take-overs involving workforce redeployment
- structural changes resulting in flatter management and multi-skilling
- the introduction of new technology
- the development of systems to improve quality

---

[2] See, for instance, Jackson (2000)

- the development of systems to meet applications for training and quality awards
- the development of systems to meet health and safety requirements

Old- and new-style workplaces

Consideration and comparison of workplaces of the 1950s/1960s and modern restructured workplaces shows that some workplaces of today operate in much the same way as the 'old-style' workplaces prior to the 1970s. These workplaces are sometime referred to as Fordist, or 'traditional' workplaces.

Others have adopted new work practices to increase their competitive edge through quality initiatives and high performance restructured workforces. New-style workplaces are sometimes termed 'high performance' or 'fast capitalist'.

Most of us are familiar with the language of old-style workplaces. Although much of this language is becoming obsolete in the context of the workplace of the 21st century, some organisations still talk in terms of large-scale (mass) production, clocking in, job security, rigid divisions of labour, collective contracts, pay bargaining, and craft.

Engineers of new-style workplaces aim to have resolved some of the issues associated with employment in the early middle part of the century: industrial conflict and strikes, poor quality production and waste. Managers talk of shared goals, continuous improvement, niche markets, flexibility, joint decision-making and democratic workplaces, team-players, employee development and learning organisations, flat management, customer focus and quality awards. Many jobs have been casualised and there is less job security and full-time employment.

Old-style workplaces are characterised by

- large-scale manufacturing
- large workforces

- Fordist, Taylorist (scientific management) methods of production
- management decision-making
- rigid hierarchy
- middle management layer
- management-level training only
- small work-cycles, fragmentation of work process
- rigid job descriptions
- workers 'hired from the neck down' to follow directions
- workers engaged in mechanical processes
- industrial conflict, union representation/confrontation
- jobs for life
- jobs mostly permanent and full-time
- workers predominantly white males

New-style workplaces are characterised by:

- 'fast capitalist' workplace of today; lean and mean, close to the customer
- decreased job security
- focus on quality of production
- concept of the 'learning organisation' and training at all levels
- quality awards
- high use of technology, ICT and computer-generated equipment
- restructured workplaces, reduced size of workforce
- team input, problem solving and decision making
- flat management
- mission statements', motivation, loyalty, shared goals
- upskilling, multiskilling (deskilling)
- individual contracts and weakened unions
- union co-operation rather than confrontation
- jobs often short-term contracts and/or part-time
- more women, minority ethnic, and disabled workers.

3.   Organisational culture

Expressions of culture include a common language, group boundaries, criteria for inclusion and exclusion, hierarchy, informal relationships, and systems of rewards, punishments and beliefs. Every organisation has a particular culture. This can be defined as "the philosophy or style" of an organisation, which might provide clues as to its basic assumptions and its beliefs about its mission and future.

For instance, the culture of a workplace might be democratic or autocratic. Carnevale, Gainer and Meltzer[3] suggest that the following are useful indicators of the extent to which workplaces are democratic:

- the degree to which management is **supportive** of its employees' efforts
- extent of **participative** decision-making
- degree of **trust** employees have in management
- **freedom to communicate** openly
- emphasis on **high performance goals**.

Language, literacy and numeracy providers working within industry need to understand and address the culture that exists, in order to be effective in introducing new ideas and provision. If a trainer does not fit in with the organisation culture it will be conspicuous, and confidence in the training will be lessened. This applies to the presentation of material, even the personal and professional presentation of practitioners. Early indicators of culture can be observed through the following:

- reception atmosphere
- ICT facilities and who has access to them
- physical environment
- sense of order at workspaces

---

[3] Carnevale, Gainer and Meltzer (1990)

- demographic profile of workers
- displays of staff awards, courses, social club notices
- tone of signs and messages to internal and external customers
- clarity of communications.

Subsequent observations might indicate:

- conflict or co-operation in teams
- 'hidden' issues such as how the awareness of the employer's restructuring or multi-skilling plans, or the presence of a strong smoking (or non-smoking) culture, affect staff relationships and work ethos
- The organisation's standing in the local community.

Some indicators of culture will be evident in the first few visits to the organisation. Others may not reveal themselves for several weeks. There is a number ways in which literacy and numeracy providers can learn about the organisational culture. They include the following:

Interviewing

This will occur in the first weeks of contact with the organisation, while task and skills needs analyses are being conducted. By interviewing workers at all levels of the organisation, the language, literacy and numeracy provider will learn how well the organisation's practice meets policy.

Documentation

This may include organisational internal and external promotions, management guidelines, award submissions and awards, organisational charts, induction handbooks, and training programmes. Evidence of awards or work towards Investors in People or other quality awards will be useful in identifying organisational culture.

Organisational philosophy and culture

This may also be contained in a mission statement. If there is a stated organisation philosophy, it could include beliefs about organisational goals, product quality, internal and external customers, employee rights and responsibilities, type of management leadership, communications culture in the workplace, equal opportunities and union participation. Policy documents should show how the organisation 'lives' its philosophy. The organisation's philosophy expressed in documents should, (but may not!) match the profile developed by observation and interviews. The closer that the philosophy, and the policy guidelines arising from it, is matched to practice, the more likely it is that the climate is a positive one

Organisational aims

These may or may not be expressed as a "Mission Statement". The organisation will have long- and short-term goals related to increasing productivity and, in most cases, profit. We need to be aware of current and projected organisational changes including "downsizing", quality measures, technology, product or service diversification, upskilling, multi-skilling, and staff development, as each of these will inform organisation training strategies, as well as language, literacy and numeracy training needs.

Hierarchy

Key management and supervisory staff might be displayed on an organisational chart or list (such as a phone list), with their roles and job titles. The presence (or absence) of a name badge culture is also revealing. A organisation that requires its employees to wear name badges indicating their first names may be trying to foster a culture of accountability, or of democratic management. Hierarchy will be affected by organisational restructuring, for example a move to flat management, more democratic decision-making. Often informal hierarchies cut across formal authority, and each of these chains of command need to be noted.

Communications

Communication styles will vary depending on the image the organisation wants to present. The style can be evidenced in the internal and external messages of policy statements and promotions. Tone and language used will provide further information (which may contrast with philosophy) about morale, industrial relations, power sharing. There may be a single "house style" for all communications, for example, one side of an A4 sheet.

Union involvement

Providers will need to know the attitude of the organisation to union involvement, which union or unions it is working with, and the extent of union participation the organisation encourages. For example, does the organisation have any Union Learning Representatives? What is the awareness of the organisation's union or unions of language, literacy and numeracy issues in the workplace? Union delegates need to be identified and information gathered about frequency of meetings and local issues. This will suggest possibilities for the steering committee.

More information about the role of the Union Learning Representatives and the role of the TUC in promoting language, literacy and numeracy in the workplace can be obtained from TUC Learning Services.

Media and web information

A great deal of background information can also be obtained from media and web sources. Your Local Learning and Skills Council (LLSC) should be able to give out useful information about companies in the local area. In addition useful information about an organisation may also be obtained from your local Regional Development Agency.

The organisation may also have its own website: what kind of image is it trying to present? Ensure that you distinguish between the organisation's promotional material and external assessment information when analysing sources for information about a particular organisation.

Training strategy

Many different factors help build a profile of the organisation's culture. It is particularly important to learn how management and employees view language, literacy and numeracy needs. Other training issues concern the distribution of training among employees at different levels, resource provision, release, choice, trainers previously and currently engaged, perceived training purpose, subsequent progression routes and promotion prospects.

Try to find answers to the following:

- does the organisation identify language, literacy and numeracy needs in staff appraisals?
- who does it see as needing language, literacy and numeracy training?
- are language, literacy and numeracy seen as an equal opportunities issue?
- is the organisation aware of the need to integrate language, literacy and numeracy training with other vocational training?

4. Cultural models

Steve Wilkinson and Isobel Gillespie[4] identify four cultural models in workplace training:

Benevolent Model

In this model, a patriarchal attitude on behalf of senior management is often visible. The staff are considered to be in need of general assistance beyond the context of work performance. Education programmes are considered beneficial for individuals but not necessarily for the company.

This model is most commonly found in 'old-style' workplaces.

Soft Training Model

Overall this model is the most prevalent. The company involved is very concerned that the training is relevant to the needs of workplace, but there are few structures to evaluate the impact of the training on performance. Although initial meetings are conducted at a high level in the company, the responsibility for maintaining programmes tends to fall entirely on lower level staff. They therefore feel a lack of ownership.

Hard Training Model

This model uses education to deal with specific production problems. The advantages are that a company knows what **it** wants to achieve and so can assess it. The company is aware that results can have a clear impact on production.

The Integrated Model

This model fits well with the Total Quality Management (TQM) approach, where the vision the company usually includes developing staff at all levels. The model is holistic and

---

[4] Wilkinson and Gillespie (1994) SCEC

participatory. It embraces the concept of a learning organisation, performance appraisal and career management. Benefits are assessed according to effect on production and quality, and on company culture. This model is recommended.

These latter three models are most commonly found in 'New Style' workplaces.

Type of provision

A provider organisation can offer a range of types of provision depending on the language, literacy and numeracy issues that have emerged during consultation with employees and managers. An organisation can only accommodate a certain number of staff release hours for language, literacy and numeracy consultancy and training, or for any other interventions. A provider might negotiate:

- short or long discrete language, literacy or numeracy programmes (for example, two hours weekly for 20–50 weeks)
- one-one provision (for example, two hours weekly or as necessary and appropriate)
- the development of user-friendly documentation
- literacy awareness for supervisory and training personnel
- specific language, literacy and numeracy support during vocational training or organisational training (for example, health and safety)
- enterprise-based tutoring (part-time on site) encompassing a range of provision, including some or all of the above.

The details of recommended provision will not become apparent until an organisational needs analysis has taken place and issues are documented in a report to the organisation. This will preferably be presented to key personnel, for example at a meeting of a committed steering group involving all key stakeholders (staff at different levels of the organisation, union representatives, and provider representatives).

Micro and macro factors influencing workplace change

This diagram illustrates the pressures of micro and macro changes on an individual organisation. Micro changes may be considered as those that occur within an individual workplace. Macro changes are national and international pressures. All impact, in different ways, on organisational and individual language, literacy and numeracy needs in the workplace.

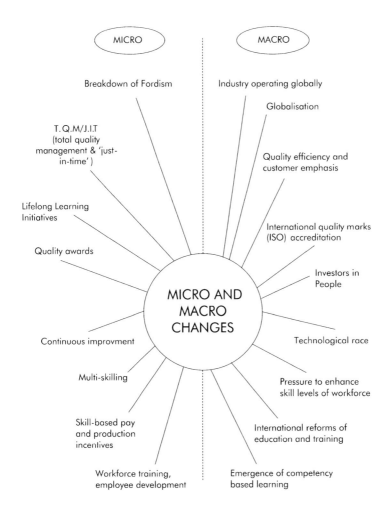

5.   New developments affecting workplace language, literacy and numeracy

Literacy and ESOL curriculum

The introduction of the new national standards in literacy and numeracy,[5] the new adult Core Curricula[6] and the mapping of Basic and Key Skills have brought about a new national framework for language, literacy and numeracy. In addition, the Basic Skills Agency has worked with many National Training Organisations (NTOs) to map the new literacy and numeracy standards to occupational standards.[7] Workplaces are more focussed on investment returns and output, and therefore tend to be more concerned with outcomes and accountability.

Union Learning Fund and Union Learning Representatives

Union Learning Representatives are a recent initiative of the TUC (Trades Union Congress). They act as mentors to encourage its members to train, including in language, literacy and numeracy in the workplace. They also reflect the more collaborative relationship of the Unions with employers and the government. The TUC is also supporting many workplace language, literacy and numeracy projects through the Union Learning Fund. The WEA (Workers' Educational Association) works collaboratively with the Trades Unions to support workplace learning, and also provide language, literacy and numeracy classes in the workplace.

---

[5] QCA 2001
[6] BSA 2001(a)
[7] BSA 2001 (b)

Ufl/Learndirect

Learndirect is a Government initiative to stimulate and meet demand for lifelong learning among businesses and individuals. Working as a public-private partnership in England, Wales and Northern Ireland, Ufl aims to put individuals in a better position to get jobs, improve their career prospects and boost business competitiveness. Learndirect's learning services provide access to innovative and high quality courses, over 80 per cent of them on-line.

Lifelong Learning Partnerships (LLPs)

Lifelong Learning Partnerships have been established sub-regionally all over England and Wales. The partnerships may comprise representatives from mainstream education, private training providers, adult and community education, and the voluntary sector. Their remit is to take a 'joined-up thinking' approach to education and training, to ensure that provision is being neither duplicated nor missed and to improve the planning and coherence of local post-16 learning. They support action to widen participation in learning, increase attainment, improve standards and meet the skills challenge, and contribute to the Government's social inclusion and regeneration agendas. They link closely with the LLSCs, providing information on regional need.

Health and Safety legislation

New Health and Safety legislation introduced in the UK since 1992 has had a major influence on the increased need for language, literacy and numeracy skills at work. This is because there is an individual legal duty on each employee to work safely, as well as increased requirements for employers. Employees need to be able to read information labels and directions, complete safety logs and accident reports, and communicate issues about safety to others. The main pieces of legislation that affect employees are:

- CoSHH (Control of Substances Hazardous to Health) 1999
- Health and Safety at Work Act 1974
- The Management of Health and Safety at Work Regulations 1992

Monitoring quality in the workplace

Total Quality Management

This is a new management style, a move from an emphasis on directly controlling people. The DTI publication on Total Quality Management and Effective Leadership[8] notes that there is "a way of managing an organisation so that every job, every process, is carried out right, first time every time. It affects everyone." It extends to visualising every function in the organisation as having a series of suppliers and customers, whether internal or external, and each person in the 'quality chain' must be aware of who their customers and their suppliers are, and continually ask themselves whether their suppliers are fully aware of their requirements, and conversely whether they are fully aware of their customers' requirements.

It further states, "If we are to define quality in a way which is useful in its management, then we must recognise the need to include in the assessment of quality, the true requirements of the 'customer' – his needs and expectations. We must then 'delight' the customer by fully meeting these needs and expectations ... the customer's needs may include performance, appearance, availability, delivery, reliability, maintainability, and cost-effectiveness ... expectations may include that the salesman is knowledgeable about the product ... [to be] treated with respect during the transaction ... Those responsible for [finding out what the customer's requirements are] must ...

---

[8] DTI (n.d.) (c)

measure ... the ability of their own organisation to meet the requirements."

SPC – Statistical Process Control[9]

Process performance is measured by gathering data (the process can be manufacturing, a service, or the transformation of information) in order to achieve and maintain a state of control and further reduce variability. It frequently requires the use of computer-controlled equipment to generate and manipulate the data.

Quality circles

"A quality circle is a team of four to 12 people usually coming from the same work area who voluntarily meet on a regular basis to identify, investigate, analyse and solve their work-related problems. The team presents its solutions to management and is then involved in implementing and monitoring the effectiveness of the solutions.

Quality Circles should be seen as part of an operations programme of continuous improvement which is often referred to as Total Quality Management."[10]

Awards

Organisations can achieve quality awards for high performance and for training. Employers are motivated to gain recognition for attention to quality, as this raises their standing with customer organisations locally, nationally and internationally.

ISO 9000 / BS EN ISO 9000[11]

This is "an international standard for quality systems" and is recognised worldwide. It was previously known as BS 5750 in

---

[9] DTI (n.d.) (d)
[10] DTI (n.d) (a)
[11] ISO (2001)

the UK, but the name was changed to reflect better its international status, when the Standard was revised during Summer 1994. A quality system is a "common-sense, business management system which can be applied to all business sectors".[12]

The implications of BS EN ISO 9000 for language, literacy and numeracy courses are that all tasks are documented, and documenting each job often comes down to the individual worker. As the written procedure for each task has to be adhered to, more reading and writing are necessary. The standard is continually reviewed. In 2001 it has been updated to include expanded detail on human resources.

PQASSO

The Practical Quality Assurance Scheme for Small Organisations is a more 'user friendly' quality assurance system and is often used by very small organisations and by voluntary and community organisations, where the ethos is more concerned with people relationships, rather than economic output. Organisations assess themselves against the PQASSO standards to prove to service users and funders that the organisation is providing a quality service. In addition some Local Authorities are using it as a model to help organisations meet the requirements of Best Value reviews, and as a base for capacity-building programmes supported by European Social Funding initiatives.

Investors in People (IiP)

The Investors in People award, administered by Local Learning and Skills Councils, is given to companies who show a commitment from the top to develop all employees to meet business objectives, to review training and development needs of all employees and to take necessary action to train. It is continuously reviewed. The development of workers'

---

[12] BSI (1994)

language, literacy and numeracy is now a recognised part of an IiP plan of action.

Basic Skills Agency post-16 Quality Mark

Organisations delivering language, literacy and numeracy in a post-16 context can apply for this recognition of the quality of their language, literacy and numeracy courses. The post-16 Quality Mark was first launched in 1992. This award focused mainly on entitlement; what anyone joining a language, literacy and numeracy programme should expect to get.

The Basic Skills Agency has now revised its original Quality Mark for organisations working with adults, so that it focuses on effectiveness as well as entitlement. The new Basic Skills Quality Mark is intended to provide a framework for raising standards of English language, literacy and numeracy among adults. Getting the Quality Mark does not depend, however, on the attainment in language, literacy and numeracy of people joining an organisation's programmes.[13]

The development of a national policy and strategy in adult language, literacy and numeracy

The Moser Report, the Adult Basic Skills Strategy Unit and Skills for Life

The Moser Report *A Fresh Start: Improving Literacy and Numeracy* (the report of the Working Group on Post-School Language, literacy and numeracy, headed by Lord Moser, 1999) included far-reaching recommendations on the funding, curriculum, accreditation, assessment and organisation of workplace, family, and community literacy and numeracy training programmes. It recommended a new system of training for adult language, literacy and numeracy practitioners, and a

---

[13] BSA (1998)

ten-fold increase in the number of language, literacy and numeracy students receiving training.

As a result of the Moser Report, a number of new initiatives were set up during the year 2000, including:

- *tutor training* for adult language, literacy and numeracy practitioners
- the 'Basic Skills Quality initiative', run by the Further Education Funding Council
- new *initial training* and *qualifications* for adult language, literacy and numeracy practitioners
- *national standards* and new *adult literacy, numeracy and ESOL curricula* and *qualifications*
- funding for workplace language, literacy and numeracy projects, such as the Union Learning Fund (managed by the TUC) and the "Building Basic Skills in the Workplace" Initiative (managed by the Workplace Basic Skills Network)
- the development of new *qualifications* and *tests*
- changes to the inspection framework for adult language, literacy and numeracy
- a new language, literacy and numeracy curriculum for adults.

Two Government-led structures also came out of the consultation process:

- a new **Cabinet Committee** on literacy and numeracy, headed by David Blunkett, Secretary of State for Education and Employment; and
- a new **Adult Basic Skills Strategy Unit** within the Department for Education and Employment, set up to deliver the Government's Adult Literacy and Numeracy Strategy.

The National Strategy

As outlined in *Skills for Life: The National Strategy for Improving Adult Literacy and Numeracy Skills*, the stated goal of the National Strategy is to:

- raise the standard of provision
- engage and motivate potential learners
- ensure that all those involved in literacy and numeracy are working towards a common goal.

A section on "low-skilled people in employment" (pp 22-25)[14] discusses involving 'employer and industry representatives, unions, the Learning and Skills Council, the Small Business Service, national training organisations, and of course large and small businesses themselves, to produce literacy and numeracy policies that address business needs as well as those of the learners'.

The document stresses that the Government will:

- **'ensure** that Information, Advice and Guidance Partnerships can help employers identify literacy and numeracy skills needs among their staff and provide advice on appropriate skills training opportunities in the local area'
- **promote** the use of clear language in companies' internal and external publications and
- support the strategy by a **'targeted promotional and information campaign** which can be used and adapted by employers themselves'.

The document talks about literacy and numeracy provision needing to be "integrated into companies' own human resources strategy" (p24) and the importance of setting up group training arrangements to encourage larger companies to open up their own training facilities to smaller local firms. "Brokers", and trade union learning representatives, are

---

[14] DfEE, 2001

acknowledged as effective motivators. Inspection measures are highlighted as a way of ensuring quality among providers.[15]

National Learning Targets for England for 2002[16]

"The National Learning Targets were launched in October 1998 to underpin departmental priorities: a globally competitive economy, with successful firms operating in a fair and efficient labour market, and a society where everyone has an equal chance to realise their potential" (Source, *DfEE National Learning Targets Annual Report*, 1998/1999). Current targets for 2002 are:

Young people

- 85 per cent of 19-year-olds to have a level 2 qualification*
- 60 per cent of 21-year-olds to have a level 3 qualification*

  * *"level 2" means 5 GCSEs at A*-C, or an NVQ level 2, or an Intermediate GNVQ (or the equivalent);"level 3" means 2 A levels, or an NVQ level 3, or an Advanced GNVQ (or the equivalent).*

Adults*

- 50 per cent of adults to have a level 3 qualification*
- 28 per cent to have a level 4 qualification*
- a 7 per cent reduction in non-learners (the Learning Participation Target*)

  * *"Adults" means all those, between the ages of 18 and 59/64, who are in employment or actively seeking employment; "level 3" means 2 A levels, or an NVQ level 3, or an Advanced GNVQ (or the equivalent); "level 4" means NVQ level 4, (having a degree or a higher level vocational qualification); and "the Learning Participation Target" covers everyone aged 16-69, except those in full-time continuous education. The target embraces all types of formal education regardless of whether they lead to a qualification.*

---

[15] Frank, 2001
[16] DfES http://dfes.gov.uk/nlt

Organisations

- 45 per cent of medium-sized or large organisations* to be recognised as Investors in People
- 10,000 small organisations* to be recognised as Investors in People

  * "Medium-sized or large organisations" means organisations with 50 or more employees; "small organisations" means organisations with 10 to 49 employees.

Key agencies

The Workplace Basic Skills Network is the only organisation in the UK specialising in workplace language, literacy and numeracy. It is a membership organisation based at Lancaster University and established in 1993. It has been funded by the DfES since 1999 to increase professional capacity in workplace language, literacy and numeracy through Continuing Professional Development, networking and support. It has managed and supported a DfES-funded delivery initiative, the "Building Basic Skills in the Workplace Initiative". It is working to research practitioner professional development need, and to develop and deliver introductory, advanced and postgraduate level Continuing Professional Development. It also works with individual provider organisations and practitioners, with a range of agencies in the UK including Regional Development Agencies and Local Learning and Skills Councils, and with European and international organisations and researchers, to build and maintain effective networks and to develop research in the field.

The Basic Skills Agency is the national development organisation for literacy and numeracy in England and Wales. It has developed a number of programme initiatives for training providers which relate to workplace provision. These include the Basic Skills Brokerage scheme, which is aimed at engaging employers through a network of trained Brokers.

Another initiative involves working with NTOs to map language, literacy and numeracy standards to the sectors' occupational standards, which are used to develop customised training programmes and materials which are used with and delivered to target groups of employees.

Progression information for practitioners

The National Training Organisation for Further Education (FENTO) has developed a set of professional standards that all new Initial Teacher Training programmes for further education must adhere to. All new practitioners entering FE need to work towards gaining one of these qualifications. New qualifications for training providers working in the non-FE sector will also replace the current Training and Development Lead Body (TDLB).

The progression pathways diagram in the Appendix gives an overview of the relationships between the new language, literacy and numeracy standards and curricula, and the FENTO professional standards for teaching and learning.

The basic skills framework diagram in the Appendix gives an overview of the relationships between the new Basic Skills Standards and Curricula and the FENTO Professional Standards for Teaching and Learning.

Making it happen

Objectives

Programme participants will be able to:

- distinguish between organisational tasks involving language, literacy and numeracy, and individual needs

- complete a training needs analysis based on a (simulated) skills audit

- identify factors influencing various stakeholder perspectives

- negotiate an issue related to workplace provision with a (simulated) steering group

6. Keeping the organisation with you

When working with organisations it is vitally important that the appropriate terminology is used ("tutors", "practitioners" or "trainers"?). Most organisations will have in-house jargon and will also be sensitive to language used in publicity. This needs to be considered when writing press releases or giving an interview. Text needs to be checked with staff first. Conversely, the organisation should be aware that it needs to check press releases about training with the provider, who is likely to be more aware of sensitivity issues around students.

The students

The organisation may have training goals for its workers. Educators may also believe they know what counts as important for students. Workers are stakeholders too: information needs to be obtained directly from them about what their perceived needs are.

Workers' learning goals may concur with those of their employers, (e.g. to be able to operate new computer systems, to cope more effectively with changing documentation, to contribute to teams). However, they are likely also have goals associated with literacy outside of their working environment such as passing their driving test, helping their children with their homework, or developing new ICT skills.

There may also be some issues for workers, which cannot be addressed by training (for example, lack of knowledge of promotion routes within the organisation, issues relating to power such as racism or sexism).

It is important that workers' wider learning goals and issues be taken into account in the development of workplace provision.

Organisational and training needs

The organisation may have a range of communications issues directly or indirectly impacting on the ability of workers to perform tasks involving the use of language, literacy and numeracy. These issues may be due to rapid changes such as the introduction of new policies and practices resulting from new technology, new legislation, award requirements, higher and broader vocational skills and qualifications requirements, metrication and European currency. In some cases, organisations may have communications issues arising from insufficient awareness of cultural issues or of the need for documentation to be user friendly.

In assessing training needs, the trainer needs to understand the way in which the policies and practices of a whole organisation (for example, systems of communication, hierarchies, chain of command, structures and structural changes) can impact on workers. Often an organisation will approach a training provider because they have identified a small number of individuals as having language, literacy and numeracy needs. Language, literacy and numeracy training may therefore be seen by the organisation as 'remedial' assistance for often low-skilled workers. Asking questions of operations managers and supervisors as well as workers will result in a fuller picture of how tasks involving language, literacy and numeracy are expected to be performed, how they are actually performed, and about any organisational changes that are impacting on new performance expectations.

7.   The organisational needs analysis (ONA)

The ONA stresses the need for the whole organisation to demonstrate a commitment to the process, and does not necessarily assume that training will always be the only "solution". Its purpose is to:

- identify overall education needs, with a focus on language, literacy and numeracy
- identify needs resulting from organisational change
- recommend an appropriate strategy (such as a training programme) for meeting identified needs.

It is preferable to include as many people as possible from a range of levels and departments in the workplace so that:

- individuals and groups do not feel singled out
- commitment is gained throughout the organisation
- improvements are understood to involve both organisational and individual development.

Individuals and groups will have different perceptions of language, literacy and numeracy issues, all of which will need to be analysed.

Step 1: Work with a steering group of management, union and workers to plan ONA

You will need to work together to decide:

- how the workforce will be told about the needs assessment and what sections of the workforce will be interviewed
- how and where the assessments will take place (confidential interviews, focus groups, job shadowing)
- suitable questions.

Step 2: Conducting the Needs Assessment

(a) Conduct interviews

When ascertaining organisational and individual needs, it is important to interview people at all levels of the organisation. It is often useful to begin with *focus* interviews. These will give you an insight into the language, literacy and numeracy expectations and issues in the workplace. You will need space for 8–12 people, and to allow 45 minutes for each group. It is important to interview supervisory and front line workers separately. You can invite the groups to discuss the day-to-day requirements of the workplace including oral and written communications, numeracy and ICT. This is likely to include issues around vocational training, health and safety, customer care, and so on, as well as the requirements of the actual jobs.

It can be helpful to conduct *confidential interviews* with people who are interested in talking about their training needs. This is more time-consuming. You will need at least 30 minutes per interviewee and a private room. We recommend a semi-structured interview in which individual workers are invited to describe the day-to-day requirements of their job and their language-, literacy- and numeracy-related concerns and training needs. A written question sheet can be used to guide this process and this will aid analysis.

For both types of interview situations, ask open questions, show interest and curiosity rather than knowledge, listen carefully, respond empathetically and encourage expansion and elaboration.

Formal assessment should not form part of this initial process. If formal testing is required, say for funding purposes, this can be carried out later at the start of the programme. It is not helpful for an organisation to carry out blanket language, literacy and numeracy tests of the entire workforce or members of the workforce, for several reasons. The tests are likely to be uncontextualised and not relate to employees' immediate use of language, literacy or numeracy, nor to their interest in learning. They are likely to cause some stress, and may be viewed with suspicion by the workforce which may suspect that management is looking for redundancies among people who fail the test. Any recommendations for training made as a result of the organisational needs analysis should allow for voluntary take-up, and testing is best carried out at the stage of take-up of the training opportunity.

(b) Observe workplace practices

It will be helpful to observe and talk to people at their work by conducting floor walks and some job shadowing. Observing the equipment that is in use in the organisation (including ICT), and noting how workers use it, is an important part of the process.

(c) Analyse workplace documents

Analysing key documents that workers are expected to use or interact with may identify alternative 'solutions', other than training, for the organisation. Note suitability for target audience, appearance and layout, organisation of ideas and information, vocabulary, sentence length and structure, cultural sensitivity. An examination of documents may indicate, for instance, a need to include translation of important documents into other languages, or to re-write complex texts into "Plain English". It is also useful to look at the extent to which workplace practices reflect goals as stated in organisational documentation.

Documents will include

- **workplace routines** (work rotas, pay slips, accident reports, time sheets, leave applications and sickness reports)
- **environmental print** (signs and notices such as Health & Safety notices)
- **job-related documents** (job cards, specifications, forms, correspondence, reports, plans, orders, manuals)

- **further training documents** (study skills, note taking, skimming, scanning, locating information)
- **documents using mathematics** (charts, graphs, measurement, time sheets, pay slips, tables)

The Organisational Needs Assessment report and recommendations

You now need to interpret findings. Some strategies will be short-term and some will take longer to implement. It is important that the information reflects the needs within the organisation, but does not identify any individual in the process. An organisation may wish a provider to make very detailed proposals, or it may wish for broad areas of learning needs to be identified, so that they can then be discussed with the Steering Group or project management group and prioritised in recommendations for provision to the organisation.

The organisational needs report should contain an introduction and overview which describes the organisation and its business, and identifies how the training provider has become involved. The organisation may have commissioned some reports itself, following the identification of a language, literacy and numeracy 'problem' at the workplace. Others will be produced by the training providers as part of a marketing exercise, and may be offered as a free service, if the training is subsequently taken up. These different approaches will dictate the overall tone of the organisational/training needs analysis (ONA/TNA) report. The report should identify the number and distribution of workers and how the data collection has taken place. The data from all workers interviewed will need to be collated for an overall picture of general skills needs. Again, samples can be useful guides.

It is important that the information reflects the needs within the organisation, but does not identify any individual in the process. The report should also make recommendations for a customised training programme that meets these needs. An organisation may wish a provider to make very detailed proposals, or it may wish for broad areas of learning needs to be identified, so that they can then be discussed with the Steering Group or project management group and prioritised in recommendations for training programmes.

Key features of an organisational needs report:

- Background to project, with acknowledgements to organisation, funders, and so on
- Explanation of ONA procedure
- Findings
- Recommendations.

Present the findings to your steering group, and gain commitment from the organisation for financial and other resources to carry out agreed action. (Try to get agreement on both short and longer term goals.)

It is important to investigate what support a worker will have with their learning. It will be difficult for a worker to complete a programme successfully if their line manager is unsupportive. This process also involves identifying any potential barriers to learning at this stage and designing the programme to address these. For example, if a line manager is likely to be unsupportive because of concerns about production figures then it will be important for the managing director and those below to show commitment to the learning programme, and to agree an organisational 'position' towards such difficulties, before the programme is commissioned. Recommendations for timing of potential training opportunities should be included in the report: and this should avoid particularly busy production periods where appropriate.

When the steering group has met to discuss the organisational needs analysis (ONA) findings and the recommendations, a programme can be promoted in the workplace. Union representatives, and particularly Union Learning Representatives, can be effective here.

8.   Negotiating with an organisation

When workplace provision is being set up it requires a good deal of negotiation between the organisation and the provider. You need to have researched the organisational hierarchy to know who to negotiate with over different issues. Negotiations have to be ongoing due to fluctations in attendance, productivity, and so on, and all parties should be kept informed.

Language, literacy and numeracy and the target group

A project may be funded by different sources with different views of whom the target group should include. For example the Local Learning and Skills Council (LLSCs) or Regional Development Agencies (RDAs) may want the target group to be "low-skilled workers", but businesses may wish to offer formal letter writing training to managers who need it. This has funding implications: "basic skills" courses may only be free up to a certain level and the company may have to pay for training above that level.

Ownership

The organisation must own the solution. If the "problem" is caused by changes in work organisation which have led to a need for language, literacy and numeracy education, the solution that is arrived at must be one that the trainer has come up with *in collaboration with* the organisation and other partners. The solution must not be imposed by the trainer without reference to organisational or worker needs.

Contracts

Organisations expect that a contract will be negotiated between all partners. If at any stage the organisation asks the trainer to do something that is not in the contract, it is important that a new/revised contract is drawn up. Regular reference to aims, expected outcomes and boundaries avoids pitfalls such as taking on more than originally negotiated.

Roles

People will have roles in relation to the project as well as their roles in the organisation. The training provider needs a clear role (advisor? facilitator?). The role of the organisation's training officer may also be complex. Have they identified the need for training and perhaps commissioned the TNA report? In this case, they may wish to maintain strategic management of the project or maintain a close 'hands-on' involvement. Alternatively, the training provider may have made contact with the managing director first of all, and the training officer may feel resentful of people from outside the organisation becoming involved.

Briefing

Who is responsible for carrying out the briefing? Have all relevant personnel been briefed? A process for managing difficult questions needs to be established.

Contact needs to be regular (weekly), clear and informative for all parties.

9. Checklist for employers considering workplace language, literacy and numeracy training

The following checklist[1] is designed to support employers new to the provision of language, literacy and numeracy in the workplace by providing a framework for the selection of suitable providers.

It provides an opportunity to gather information about the potential training providers and their capacity and experience in the workplace language, literacy and numeracy field, how far they have an understanding of sectoral issues and workplace change issues and the ability to integrate language, literacy and numeracy training with vocational training.

Quality of provider			
	Yes	**No**	**Comments**
Holds (or working towards) a Basic Skills Agency Quality Mark			
Ability to provide references from other employers			
Qualified/experienced workplace language, literacy and numeracy trained staff , for example, holding the Workplace Basic Skills Network's *Breaking Down Barriers (BDB1)* Initial Certificate in Workplace Basic Skills Training			
Inspection grades available (if applicable)			
Demonstrates commitment to equal opportunities			

---

[1] Batt and Pegum 2001

Programme provision			
	Yes	**No**	**Comments**
Able to offer a range of delivery models			
Plans for monitoring and review at regular intervals			
Able to link training to organisational need caused by, for example, technological change, legislation change, Vocational and other organisational training and structural changes			
Demonstrated previous experience of workplace language, literacy and numeracy delivery and design of customised learning resources in....			
Workplace numeracy			
Workplace communication skills, oral and written			
Workplace basic computer skills			
Workplace English for speakers of other languages			
Recruitment training			

Management of provision

	Yes	No	Comments
Able to identify a named contact/co-ordinator to take responsibility for all aspects of the activity			
Able to agree a meeting schedule with representation from provider, employer and trades unions to discuss aspect concerned with provision			
Able to agree processes and administration, including those required by external funding sources			
Able to contribute to the internal marketing of the programme			
Able to provide contextualised individual and organisational communications needs analysis			
Able to provide job skills audit			
Able to negotiate flexible and adaptable scheduling of programmes to fit with work pressures and workers' shift patterns			
Able to deliver on an organisation's premises where appropriate			
Able to respond to demand and growth			

Costs			
	Yes	No	Comments
Established links with funding providers and able to access potential sources of funding			
Able to provide costings for different models			

Evaluation of the programme			
	Yes	No	Comments
Can provide evidence of programme meeting organisational objectives and stakeholder priorities			
Can provide evidence of programme meeting individual participants' objectives.			
Can give general feedback from individual progress sheets (without disclosing individuals' progress)			

10. The steering group

There will need to be ongoing negotiations with management and staff. It is important that a project management team or *steering group*, representative of all parties, is established as early as possible. It is recommended that the group is made up of the following people:

- training provider co-ordinator and/or a programme practitioner from Training Provider organisation
- an employer manager
- the organisation training officer
- a supervisor or line manager
- a course participant
- a union representative.

The role of the steering group is to meet periodically and discuss progress and problems.

A good steering group usually leads to better communications and improved industrial relations and is often the only forum in which the needs of manual workers are discussed and focussed upon, and in which people from all levels in the organisation get together. There are very few programmes that are problem-free and it is important to have a forum in which to discuss these and decide strategies for overcoming them.

It is essential that the steering group has some ownership of the programme by participating in aspects of planning.

This could include:

- participating in goal-setting
- deciding on appropriate evaluation materials and criteria
- gathering resources and teaching materials
- monitoring problems, changes and improvements in workplace practices
- providing ongoing support for workers engaged in the programme.

The practitioner, as the representative of the training organisation, will need to set up and/or maintain regular meetings with the steering group, demonstrating a professional time-conscious approach and a willingness to share, explain, and invite comments on programme developments. The agenda for each meeting needs to be jointly negotiated and purposeful. Confidentiality of individual students' progress must be guarded.

Stakeholder perspectives

Each participant in the steering group comes with her/his own agenda, influenced by different factors and prioritising different issues. It is important that each stakeholder feels that they are involved in the project decision-making and that their perspective is respected.

Setting up the programme

One or two members of the steering group are likely to have been your first point of contact in promoting the programme, developing the organisational needs analysis and securing the contract. The wider group will now need to ensure that the programme runs smoothly. Any changes to agreements made at this and later points should be altered in the contract.

Practical details to negotiate with the steering group

Rooms/access

It may be that there is a learning centre already set up in the organisation that is ideal for training purposes. However, you may be offered a room which seems inappropriate (such as the Staff Canteen) or which does not meet the minimum levels of standards you would expect from a college venue. You may need to negotiate a suitable compromise with the organisation management, such as sharing the facilities of a sister or neighbouring organisation. Because many potential learners may initially doubt the relevance of the programme to their work, or may have negative experiences of education, deciding to hold a workplace language, literacy and numeracy programme at a college or training provider site should always be a last resort.

Release

Productivity is the main priority for managers. Providers need to be flexible and patient when dealing with release time for workers. Changing shift patterns generally cause the most difficulty, and can result in fluctuating attendance. Often the best solution is to have two sessions each week with the same content. It is wise to ensure that the managing director's decision for staff to be released regularly to attend a programme has been communicated to line management.

Content and delivery

Delivery must have a focus, yet be flexible, and have a balance in terms of job-related and non-job-related material. Relationship to NVQ accreditation should be established. Organisation goals for the training programme need to be made explicit, as do learner outcomes. All agreed decisions need to be documented.

Organisations usually expect ongoing reports on progress as provision is being delivered. These are much easier to compile when the content is well planned and meets the original aims and objectives.

Resources

Will the organisation allow you to have access to ICT facilities for all workers? Often this is a key "inclusion" issue along with ideas about access to training itself. Costing of resources should be considered carefully, so that "last minute" photocopying can be accounted for, as well as the production of worksheets. The ownership of any resources produced should also be addressed. If, for example, a trainer produces an exciting activity that enables bakery workers to practise their numeracy skills in metric conversion of ingredients, the bakery may be unhappy for this activity to be used at a later date with any of their perceived "competitors".

Disability awareness

Changes in employment and discrimination legislation mean that a language, literacy and numeracy practitioner is far more likely than previously to have learners with disabilities in a workplace programme. Some questions relating to the Disability Discrimination Act 1995 and the Special Educational Needs and Disability Act 2001, which you may need to consider, are:

- Are you able to cater for the needs of any workers with disabilities?
- Can the room be accessed with a wheelchair?
- Is there an induction loop for deaf and hard of hearing people?
- Are you able to access dyslexia assessment and support facilities for individuals who are dyslexic?
- Do any of the workers have specific or non-specific learning difficulties?

Steering Group

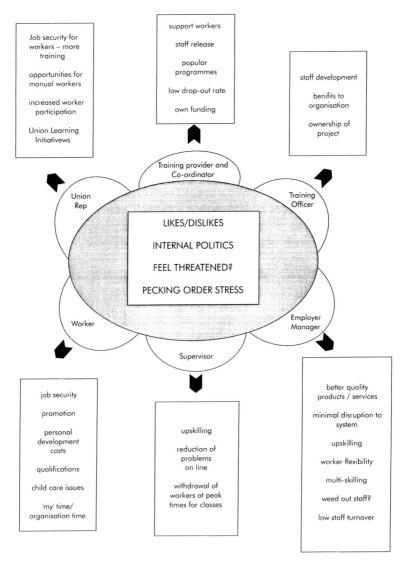

Job security for
workers – more
training

opportunities for
manual workers

increased worker
participation

Union Learning
Initiativews

---

support workers

staff release

popular
programmes

low drop-out rate

own funding

---

staff development

benifits to
organisation

ownership of
project

Training provider and
Co-ordinator

Union
Rep

Training
Officer

LIKES/DISLIKES

INTERNAL POLITICS

FEEL THREATENED?

PECKING ORDER STRESS

Worker

Employer
Manager

Supervisor

---

job security

promotion

personal
development
costs

qualifications

child care issues

'my' time/
organisation time

---

upskilling

reduction of
problems
on line

withdrawal of
workers at peak
times for classes

---

better quality
products / services

minimal disruption to
system

upskilling

worker flexibility

multi-skilling

weed out staff?

low staff turnover

Confidentiality: The key to a sustainable programme

Some general ground rules have to be set down at the start of your project as follows:

- participation is voluntary
- individual progress is confidential
- learning outcomes are reported anonymously

Checklist

- All personal or work-related information disclosed by students is confidential and should not be repeated by practitioners to anyone (not even family). If you decide to seek guidance on an issue from your own line manager, talk about process rather than personal details.
- Resist the urge to intervene on a participant's behalf. Encourage participants to problem-solve for themselves. This is more empowering than intervening on their behalf.
- If requested by a participant to intervene on that participant's behalf, seek guidance from your own line manager. If in doubt, do nothing. Remember: you are unlikely to be aware of all the factors. Your intervention may damage the participant. It may damage relations with the employer. It may damage your organisation's credibility.

Consider …

It is quite likely that practitioners may experience some of the following situations. What is your role?

- the cleaners often smoke in the storeroom where you go to talk to them. Their manager tells you he suspects this.
- your student has difficulty doing calculations on his job because his supervisor often shouts aggressively at him when he's trying to do them.
- a supervisor is overtly racist to staff in front of you.

- you are told the name of someone who is said to be stealing regularly from the back of the warehouse.
- you suspect that the employer is looking for evidence to justify sacking an worker.

Setting it up

Objectives

Programme participants will be able to:

- develop and deliver an appropriately targeted oral or written presentation

- employ Plain English principles in developing written presentations

- outline a 20-hour programme of learning for a small group

11. Publicity

Many large organisations will have a good marketing department and it can often be useful to work with this department for your needs. If this can be arranged it has the following benefits:

- the organisation house style can be easily adopted
- internal publicity is distributed quickly and easily
- ownership of the programmes is shared
- the organisation will often be quite happy to help with publicity, especially if they are involved in gaining an award such as "Investors in People".

However, if you work for an FE College, it is also likely to have a marketing department that is keen to ensure that all publicity conforms to its own house style. In both cases, it is important to liaise closely with the publicity designer to ensure that information about the programme is accurately and sensitively portrayed.

Staff development and job security

It is helpful to highlight to staff that the employer is investing in staff development. Workers will be most concerned about confidentiality and job security, so it is also important that providers clearly identify an organisation's motives, and retain full confidentiality of workers' interviews and progress. Once this understanding is reached with the organisation, the confidentiality aspect can be promoted to workers.

Publicity can be achieved in the following ways:

- by sending out a flier in each pay packet
- by putting posters around the workplace
- by sending memos to line managers
- using the staff email system
- by doing presentations to staff and managers

- by talking to staff and managers on a one-to-one basis
- by word of mouth by users
- by sending out leaflets to staff
- by attending team briefings
- by talking to people in break times
- by setting up displays and videos.

Producing a leaflet

Key points to remember...

- make it look professional
- make it easy to understand
- use language for industry not education
- sell your skills well.

White space

- It is important that anyone reading a text can find their way round easily. Too much text on a page can put people off. Columns too close together often cause confusion.
- People who find reading difficult need short, clearly separated chunks of text which they can work through at their own pace. This helps them to see how far they have to go, and reduces the chances of them giving up. Pages that have no margins, or little space between the paragraphs, are more difficult to read. In addition, left-aligned, "ragged" text is often much easier to read than justified text, particularly for people with dyslexia.

Leading

- The spacing between lines is important in making reading easier. Lines written very close together make the reading of a passage far more difficult. With normal 12pt type a 2pt leading is about right.

Type size

- The size of the type should be related to the amount of text. However, very large type maybe seen as patronising.

Page layout

- Headings and subheadings should be clear. A new line for each new statement can be more effective then cramming text.

Colour/types of paper

- Use good quality paper that is thick enough to prevent "shadowing" from the other side of the page, or glossy card. Use white or light coloured paper, as dark colours make reading more difficult.

Text

- Short statements are more effective than rambling sentences. Avoid unnecessary phrases, for example, "in order to" (to). Use direct, active language. Although readability formulae such as "SMOG" are sometimes used, they tend to be inappropriate for the workplace because of the need to include relevant technical workplace terms in a poster or leaflet. This may then give an incorrect impression that the "pitch" of the text is too high.

Graphics

- Pictures, logos, photographs and clipart all help to attract attention and convey meaning; and may also be particularly useful where workers have significant ESOL needs. However, take care when using clipart that very simple pictures are not seen to trivialise the message.

12. The programme outline

In developing a learning programme, the practitioner needs to:

- identify and explicitly state learning objectives as they relate to skills required on the job
- acknowledge workers as independent thinkers with prior knowledge and experience, and include students in the decision-making process on the content of the programme
- integrate with other vocational training where appropriate
- enlist the steering group in setting the goals of the programme, and monitoring and discussing its progress.
- take account of any potential barriers to learning (such as production issues, childcare) when designing the structure of the programme.

Ten steps in designing the programme

- Use negotiated training priorities as the basis of the programme.
- Establish hours of instruction per week, and number of weeks available (check for public holidays, expected production rushes, shift problems).
- Ensure that a suitable training room (space, lighting) with appropriate resources is available (may include whiteboard, overhead projector, computer(s), access to photocopier).
- Outline possible objectives, outcomes and criteria for evaluation of learning and discuss with steering group (realistic, achievable?). Discuss integration with vocational training opportunities.
- Promote programme to workforce.
- Conduct recruitment interviews and select initial group of students (establish that there is a further option for other interested employees).
- Decide on curriculum (map to accreditation), teaching materials and delivery methods.

- Collect additional suitable workplace materials to be used as instructional materials.
- Implement programme.
- Meet with steering group throughout the programme to ensure needs of all stakeholders are being met, and to evaluate progress.

All of these components are interrelated, and depend on thorough preparatory steps (training needs analysis, effective steering group negotiations, careful recruitment, materials gathering, and so on).

13. Delivery options

Short workplace-based programmes

This is the most usual option. Typically programmes are run for between ten and 14 weeks, with a 2-4 hourly session once a week. Although the sessions are short, they can disrupt production if they include a number of workers from the same process/team. Classes may be held in meeting rooms, lunchrooms or even unused work bays. They are not generally integrated with other training such as health and safety, or with daily routines such as meetings. However, they may be integrated with other vocational training programmes such as NVQs, by providing additional learning support.

Ten to 18 weeks is the optimum length of time for a short programme. It does not seem too overwhelming for a student new to learning. However, if the programme is accredited in its own right, it may cause problems by providing insufficient time to develop portfolios. If the programme is integrated with other vocational training programmes, or has been developed as a highly customised programme for a particular workplace, or industry, it is less likely to be accredited. Currently the Government is piloting intensive "one day a week for 13 weeks" programmes for employees, paying employers for staff release time. More details about this can be found in the national strategy document for adult literacy and numeracy, *Skills for Life* (DfEE 2001).

College-based programmes

These are generally run over a longer period. Workers attend during or outside of work hours with workers from other organisations. Practitioners may have little contact with workplace personnel and workers may feel that the programme is not relevant to their needs.

Employee development schemes

In an employee development scheme, full or part time training personnel are usually employed by the organisation, or may be seconded from a college. This allows for greater accessibility and flexibility. A part of the workplace is designed especially for a range of learning activities determined by a committee from workers' suggestions. Learning occurs in workers' time and provision options include language, literacy and numeracy. The most well-known of these centres is the EDAP (Employee Development and Assistance Programme) scheme at Ford's car manufacturing plant.

Enterprise-based practitioners

These practitioners are contracted to an organisation through a language and literacy provider for part of the week. They work in a training area which they may share with the organisation's trainer or other contracted providers.

They are in a good position to develop language and literacy provision which is integrated with organisational developments and training. Their role is to provide individual learning support on site (sometimes at the production line), to run programmes for groups, and to assist management with communications issues such as developing user-friendly documentation.

Developing the learning programme

Objectives

Participants will:

- be able to state some of the key ingredients and guiding principles for framing basic skills training programmes

- demonstrate the ability to map samples of workplace materials to national accreditation

- gain an understanding of students' and others' expectations of courses

- relate a course outline to workers' issues and interests and incorporate relevant accredited units

- critically evaluate existing evaluation methods and design their own

14. Developing objectives and learning outcomes

Aims

The "aim" of a workplace programme is the general statement about what the course is designed to achieve. For example, the aim of a workplace language, literacy and numeracy programme for day care centre workers might be: "The programme will enable the participants to improve their paper-work and inter-personal skills in the day care centre".

Objectives

Objectives are specific (often activity-based) targets that are designed to be achieved, often within a single session. There should also be evidence (for example, written notes, oral contribution, answering a question) of how they have been achieved. An example of a workplace basic skills programme objective might be: "In this session participants will practise completing an accident report form." Objectives are SMART:

S – specific
M – measurable
A – achievable
R – realistic
T – targeted

Learning outcomes

Learning outcomes may be thought of as the result of the objectives of a course being met. They express what a partici-pant might be expected to *know* or *do* as a result of attending the programme. Many competence-based courses focus on learning outcomes, rather than objectives, as this does not prescribe the manner in which the participant's knowledge, skills or understanding is to be acquired.

Developing clear objectives and learning outcomes is important for evaluation purposes (have you delivered what you promised?) and for accreditation purposes. If you are considering accrediting your programme you will need to be able to identify the objectives and learning outcomes, in order to be able to match them to the requirements of the awarding body.

Accrediting workplace programmes

Many workers may be keen to undertake an accredited course in order to gain a certificate as recognition for their achievements. Similarly employers may also be keen for their workers to achieve a recognised qualification, in order to provide evidence towards a quality mark such as Investors in People.

However, many employers are not interested in an accredited course; perhaps because they do not value a basic skills qualification certificate, or because the prescriptive nature of an accredited course may conflict with their desire to support a highly customised course for their particular industry. If an employer would like an accredited course then the following systems are useful.

New Adult Literacy and Numeracy Core Curricula

The Adult Literacy Core Curriculum and the Adult Numeracy Core Curriculum documents were developed by the Basic Skills Agency, the Qualifications and Curriculum Authority and the Adult Basic Skills Strategy Unit in 2000. They are intended to be used a *guide* for teachers of basic skills on teaching methods and activities. Accrediting bodies are mapping their qualifications to this framework.

City & Guilds

The City and Guilds qualifications in literacy and numeracy are designed to allow tutors to choose contexts which are relevant to their students' needs and aspirations and to demonstrate competence in a range of communication activities. City and Guilds strongly recommend that the activities used to achieve the competencies described in the units and elements should be real. At the time of writing the most commonly used City and Guilds qualifications in basic skills are Wordpower and Numberpower.

National Open College Network

This is a national network of awarding bodies which offer a range of qualifications. Qualifications may be undertaken by fulfilling the requirements of existing units in their qualifications databank, in order to best meet the needs of workers. Alternatively, if a tutor has designed a particular workplace programme that has been used successfully, and wishes to use it again, s/he may wish to consider having the course accredited by their local Open College network. This can then offer some of the advantages of accreditation for workers (such as gaining a certificate) without compromising industry relevance.

A tutor will need to consider other objectives and learning outcomes in the design of the course. It may be that a workplace language, literacy and numeracy course will be integrated with other vocational training at the workplace, and the training a tutor provides is concerned with enabling workers to meet the language, literacy and numeracy requirements of an NVQ portfolio. Learning objectives here may concentrate on empowering workers to meet other accreditation requirements, rather than specifying particular basic skills components that will be addressed throughout the programme.

There is a large number of accredited programmes and awarding bodies, and practitioners should familiarise themselves with the options that are available and most appropriate for their particular context.

Workplace resources

Workplace documents and procedures should be used in the language, literacy and numeracy courses wherever possible. Examples are form-filling and using reference systems, workplace accident forms, stocktaking forms, giving and following procedural instructions, interpreting and giving clear written and oral messages, completing records and telephone message forms. These provide relevant vehicles for practising transferable skills as workers can transfer knowledge and skills gained about the language and forms of their job to other contexts.

15. Accreditation in the workplace context

Advantages of accreditation	Disadvantages of accreditation
For workers: • gaining a certificate – may be the first qualification that the worker has ever gained • recognition of progress • certificate may have currency for future training opportunities	For workers: • a basic skills certificate may have no currency in the current workplace or in applying for jobs in the future. • it may be difficult to complete course requirements in the time available • may act as disincentive if some workers cannot complete the course
For employers: • may be able to access external funding for an accredited programme • accredited courses may provide evidence towards liP • workers may be more enthusiastic about undertaking an accredited programme	For employers: • an accredited programme may be too inflexible and prescriptive • there may be insufficient time available to complete the portfolio • employers may not recognise value of a 'basic skills' certificate as opposed to other forms of vocational training

Mapping to accreditation

It is important to map the accreditation to the workplace programme and not the other way round. Workers should not be required to undertake inappropriate activities in order to meet learning outcomes. A tutor should be able to look at opportunities for accreditation of prior learning (APL) in the workplace. Communication Skills Entry Level and Level One can provide units and elements to which workplace learning can be mapped turn, these skills and competencies may be mapped to National Vocational Qualifications.

For instance, where an Entry Level element requires the student to "extract information from a graphical source" and the needs analysis has determined that graph reading should be included in the curriculum, then the student can achieve that element.

This table can be used to help identify the links between task components and accreditation elements

Activities involved in the job/task (can you use these as a learning resource, or can you APL existing skills?)	
Language, literacy and numeracy components (are there any transferable skills included in the task?)	
Accreditation element (where appropriate)	

National Qualifications Framework[1]

Schools	Adult Core Curriculum	Key Skills	National Qualification Framework
		Key Skills Level 5	National Qualifications Framework Level 5
		Key Skills Level 4	National Qualifications Framework Level 4
	Adult Core Curriculum	Key Skills Level 3	National Qualifications Framework Level 3
Schools	Literacy / Numeracy Level 2	Key Skills Level 2	National Qualifications Framework Level 2
National Curriculum Level 5 / National Curriculum Level 4	Literacy / Numeracy Level 1	Key Skills Level 1	National Qualifications Framework Level 1
National Curriculum Level 3	Literacy / Numeracy Entry Level 3		
National Curriculum Level 2	Literacy / Numeracy Entry Level 2		Entry Level
National Curriculum Level 1	Literacy / Numeracy Entry Level 1		

[1] Source: Qualifications and Curriculum Authority 2001

16. Programme expectations

It is important to balance the expectations of all the stake-holders involved in the workplace basic skills programme.

Workplace students' expectations may include:

❏ being able to do their current job better
❏ being able to progress to a better job
❏ being able to do their current training programme more effectively
❏ ability to access leisure courses:
❏ to help children with homework
❏ to write letters/read books
❏ to undertake writing/reading connected with hobbies

The organisation's expectations may include:

❏ reduced wastage or frequency of errors
❏ improved staff morale
❏ increased willingness of staff to undertake further vocational training or promotion opportunities
❏ being able to achieve or maintain IiP status

The training provider's expectations may include:

❏ meeting the agreed outcome targets of the course
❏ making a profit
❏ being commissioned to run further courses
❏ evidencing a high satisfaction rating from the workplace students on the course.

Are there any other stakeholders who may have expectations from the course?

The stakeholders may have different ideas about progression outcomes from the course. As a training provider, you should be prepared to provide information on:

❏ local general education courses for students to do in their own time

❏ in-house vocational qualifications which students will be able to access after the courses: the City & Guilds course 7324/03 (Basic Skills Support in the Workplace) offers some useful guidelines

❏ other programmes and courses which you offer

❏ information on courses that may be offered by other training providers

❏ how to progress within a qualification that the worker has already taken eg Wordpower level 1 to Wordpower level 2

❏ other general contact information that will enable the worker to make an informed choice about their own progression goals. Examples of contact details you may be asked for include: The local College, the local Learndirect centre, childcare providers, Union or WEA contacts, the Citizens Advice Bureau, Community centres, and so on.

17. Evaluation

Evaluation must involve all stakeholders in the workplace, at the early planning stage of a programme. It is vital to be clear about what should be evaluated, how, and what would count as evidence. Those involved should be prepared for, and welcome, issues revealed, as they can be used to inform and improve future provision and practice.

Evaluation occurs during several phases of the setting up of a programme, as well as during and after delivery. For instance, learning needs are evaluated in the Training recruitment phases, and re-assessed during the initial stages of programme delivery. Initial assessment of workers' learning needs in the early stage of the programme is also a form of evaluation

Formative evaluation
This takes place during the beginning and middle stages of programme operation. The purpose is to identify issues which can be addressed and modified while change is still possible and productive for the current cohort.

Summative evaluation
Usually takes place at the end of programme operation and is designed to measure how well the programme has succeeded.

Typical goals:

- improved learner language, literacy and numeracy abilities
- improved language, literacy and numeracy practices at work and elsewhere
- improved learner productivity at work

Assessment can be through:

- informally constructed tests related to the workplace
- questionnaires related to basic skills practices

- informal discussion with workers
- one-to-one interviews with learners and supervisors
- learning logs
- formal standardised texts
- accreditation objectives.

Summative evaluations need to review much more than delivery, student participation, satisfaction and performance. Other important considerations include:

- planning
- needs assessment
- recruitment procedures
- curriculum design
- appropriateness of content
- appropriateness and use of materials
- facilities and resources
- long-term impact on the workplace
- suitability of programme length/duration of sessions
- impact on the wider community ('inter-generational' factors, increased involvement in community activities by participants/improved self-confidence).
- informal and formal feedback from participants, supervisors and management
- records of training needs analysis, steering group meetings, course recruitment and planning, student progress
- documentation of changes in workplace performance (performance appraisals)
- documentation of changes in morale, promotion and further training participation

Remember the importance of

- Confidentiality
- The need to use positive language
- Using appropriate, non-complex language

Parts of evaluation instruments can be standard for all programmes, but much needs to be custom designed for each programme. Samples used in other workplace settings can provide useful guides in developing evaluation tools and methodology for new programmes. A number of publications (for example, Rees 1990) provide useful examples. There are many different ways to design a questionnaire but the following considerations could be borne in mind when designing a questionnaire for a workplace language, literacy and numeracy programme.

Questionnaire design

Does the design of your questionnaire:

- Reflect the needs of a specific workplace programme?
- Use appropriate language for the intended audience ?
- Ask relevant questions that will provide with the information you want to know?
- Address the issues and priorities of all stakeholders in the workplace programme?
- Use a mix of quantitative and qualitative questions?
- Ensure that the layout is clear and easy to read?
- Address issues of purpose and confidentiality?
- Avoid the use of middle scoring responses, by designing response rating systems in sets of 4, 6, or 8?
- Thank employees for taking part?

Accreditation information

Unit One

General concepts of workplace language, literacy and numeracy training and organisational culture

Suggested assignment for 1.1
Suggested assignment for 1.2

Unit Two

Making it happen

Suggested assignment for 2.1
Suggested assignment for 2.2

Unit Three

Setting it up

Suggested assignment for 3.1
Suggested assignment for 3.2

Unit Four

Developing the learning programme

Suggested assignment for 4.1
Suggested assignment for 4.2

Summary record sheet

Unit One: General concepts of workplace language, literacy and numeracy

Identify recent organisational trends and their impact on organisational culture and training

Suggested assignment for 1.1

Provide a brief explanation for changes in organisational structures, systems and practices in recent decades, and discuss how such changes impact on workers today.

Element 1.1

Demonstrates knowledge of organisational change and of how these changes have impacted on workers.

Performance criteria

Has described and explained how and why organisations have changed in terms of:

- philosophy, policy, goals
- chain of command
- production
- industrial relations
- employee decision-making
- division of labour
- job security

Evidence indicators

Displays an understanding of:

- the forces that have shaped organisational change over the last two decades

- the impact these changes have had on basic skills in the workplace
- the enhanced role of workplace training

Evidence requirements
A written assignment demonstrating an understanding of the ways organisations have changed and the implications this has for workplace basic skills training

Suggested assignment for 1.2
Develop a case study of a real company and report on how the culture of this organisation impacts on its attitude towards workplace language, literacy and numeracy training.

Element 1.2
Identify how the culture of a company is related to its language, literacy and numeracy training policy.

Performance criteria
Has discussed in the context of this organisation:

- how current quality requirements (eg. awards, legislation, vocational training) impact on current operational practices
- how these practices have impacted on its language, literacy and numeracy skills
- changes in company recruitment patterns

Evidence indicators
Displays an understanding of:

- the concept of company culture
- the company's attitude to "basic skills" training

Evidence requirements
A written report on the relationship of an organisation's culture and attitude towards workplace language, literacy and numeracy training.

Unit Two: Making it happen

Identify basic skills learning needs and negotiate provision with the organisation

Suggested assignment for 2.1

Develop an organisational report based on an interview/assessment. Distinguish between work tasks, language, literacy and numeracy components and workers' needs.

Element 2.1

Develop a Language/Literacy/Numeracy Training Report

Performance criteria

Has produced an Organisational Needs Analysis report:

- mapping basic skills components to job tasks and detailing individual basic skills needs
- outlining the difference between task analysis, language, literacy and numeracy components and workers' actual basic skills needs
- a proposal for meeting needs based on the organisational needs analysis.

Evidence indicators

Displays an understanding of:

- different types of workplace language, literacy and numeracy practices (eg. routines and procedures, written notices, oral communications)
- the differences between job tasks, language, literacy and numeracy components and workers' actual needs

Demonstrates:

- the ability to assess the training needs of a group of workers

Evidence requirements
Completed organisational needs analysis report containing sections on:

- background information about the organisation
- the needs analysis process (job tasks, language, literacy and numeracy components, workers' skills needs)
- findings (needs identified)
- training recommendations

Suggested assignment for 2.2

Participate, in role, in a meeting of organisation and basic skills training stakeholders, for the purpose of addressing a basic skills training issue. Contribute to the issue's resolution from your role position. Comment on stakeholder perspectives and issues around the process of negotiation.

Element 2.2
Negotiate workplace language, literacy and numeracy training issues taking account of various stakeholders' agendas and perspectives.

Performance criteria
Has

- identified the concerns and priorities of personnel in a basic skills steering group meeting
- identified the key workplace training issues following discussion with the group
- taken account of the differing concerns, priorities and issues of stakeholders
- evaluated the negotiation process and identified appropriate solutions

Evidence indicators

Displays an understanding of:

- workplace training issues
- stakeholders' perspectives on the issues
- the negotiation process
- effective solutions reached

Evidence requirements

- Video- or audio-taped recording of your participation in a simulated exercise
- Evidence of your contribution to an agreed solution
- Evaluation of the meeting, reflecting on general issues, stakeholders' perspectives, conflict and negotiation.

Unit Three: Setting it up

Promote provision to employees and design a programme outline

Suggested assignment for 3.1

Either

Plan and produce a leaflet or poster which is sensitive and readable for a specific worker target audience. Use this poster to discuss how you would encourage employees to take up basic skills provision. Show how your leaflet/poster would complement an overall positive promotional strategy for workplace basic skills.

or

Plan and implement an address to a group (approximately five minutes) on the proposed programme. Show how your address would complement an overall positive promotional strategy for workplace basic skills.

Element 3.1

Promote language, literacy and numeracy training in the workplace, as part of a positive promotional strategy to workers, and discuss.

Performance criteria

Has produced *either*:

- a notice/leaflet as part of a positive promotional strategy to workers about a proposed programme, and discussion

or

- an address as part of a positive promotional strategy to employees to promote a proposed programme, and evaluative discussion

Evidence indicators

Displays an understanding of:

- what should be regarded as essential information
- the appropriate tone for the communication
- the need for clarity
- how this work complements an overall promotional strategy to workers
- a positive promotional strategy based on an enhancement rather than deficit model of basic skills

Evidence requirements

- Effective, sensitive and appropriately targeted leaflet completed and discussed as part of an overall positive strategy

or

- Presentation requirements met, and written evaluative discussion of how the presentation would complement an overall positive strategy

Suggested assignment for 3.2

Design 20 hours of a programme for a group identified in an organisational needs analysis. List course objectives. Include references to work contexts and tasks where appropriate. Take account of worker interests, and include at least one sample activity.

Element 3.2

Design a workplace language, literacy and numeracy programme based on negotiations with workers and management which shows an understanding of good adult teaching practice.

Performance criteria

Has produced a workplace basic skills programme containing

- clear aims and objectives
- content and materials appropriate to the needs of workers and citizens
- appropriate adult teaching and learning methods
- activities specifically related to the workplace in question

Evidence indicators

Evidence that the design of the programme has taken account of the need for

- realistic aims and objectives
- a content and materials that are attractive to, and meet the needs of, participants
- teaching and learning methods that are appropriate to the audience
- a balance between employer and worker objectives.

Evidence requirements

- an outline of the whole programme
- individual session plans listing, objectives, materials, activities, etc.
- reference to national adult literacy, numeracy, ESOL standards and curriculum guidelines
- at least one sample activity.

Unit Four: Developing the learning programme
Working with assessment and evaluation

Suggested assignment for 4.1

Outline accreditation options and map, where appropriate, basic skills elements for a planned workplace language, literacy and numeracy programme. Discuss the opportunities and limitations for workers in regard to accrediting workplace language, literacy and numeracy learning.

Element 4.1

Outline accreditation options, and map, where appropriate, elements in a planned workplace language, literacy and numeracy programme. Show an understanding of the advantages, limitations and problems for workers in regard to accrediting workplace language, literacy and numeracy.

Performance criteria

- has demonstrated a knowledge of existing accreditation frameworks and options
- has mapped, where appropriate, accreditation criteria, Adult Literacy and Numeracy Core Curriculum guidelines, National Standards levels in Adult Literacy and Numeracy, and National Occupational Standards, to a planned workplace language, literacy and numeracy programme
- has noted some advantages for workers in accrediting their learning

Evidence indicators

Displays an understanding of at least two of the following:

- ways in which accreditation criteria, Adult Literacy and Numeracy Core Curriculum guidelines, National Standards

levels in Adult Literacy and Numeracy, and National Occupational Standards can be mapped to a planned workplace language, literacy and numeracy programme
- some limitations and problems with current accreditation frameworks, related to operational constraints and learning circumstances of workers
- opportunities for linking to APL, vocational training and progression

Evidence requirements
A written discussion of accreditation issues for workers, including a mapping of elements in a planned workplace language, literacy and numeracy programme to at least one of the following: accreditation criteria, Adult Literacy and Numeracy Core Curriculum guidelines, National Standards levels in Adult Literacy and Numeracy, or National Occupational Standards.

Suggested assignments for 4.2

Either
Produce an appropriate evaluation form for workers who have completed a workplace language, literacy and numeracy programme at entry level one/level two of the National Standards in Adult Literacy and Numeracy or a nationally recognised accreditation scheme, and justify its question content and design.

or
Design and produce an alternative evaluation method, which does not rely on a written questionnaire, and justify its question content and design.

Element 4.2
Produce an effective and appropriate evaluation method for workers.

Performance criteria

The evaluation form has:

- identified the appropriate language and approach for work-place evaluation
- takes into account personal and work-related content, process and outcomes
- asked useful questions effectively

The alternative evaluation method has:

- provided the rationale for an alternative evaluation method
- designed an appropriate evaluation method taking into account personal and work-related content, process and outcomes
- asked useful questions effectively

Evidence indicators

Displays a knowledge of

- appropriate evaluation tools for workplace programmes which will provide valid evidence for improving programmes

Evidence requirements

Either:

An appropriate workplace evaluation form, and a justification for its question content and design

or:

An alternative method of evaluation for the workplace and a justification for its question content and design.

Assessment record sheet

Student: **Tutor:**

General concepts Unit 1 Element 1.1 Element 1.2		
Making it happen Unit 2 Element 2.1 Element 2.2		
Setting it up Unit 3 Element 3.1 Element 3.2		
Developing the learning programme Unit 4 Element 4.1 Element 4.2		

Further comments and recommendations

Bibliography and further reading

Batt, S and Pegum, S (2001) *Checklist for Employers considering Language, Literacy and Numeracy Training*, Workplace Basic Skills Network

BSA (1994) *Basic Skills Support in Business and Industry*, Basic Skills Agency, London

BSA (1994) *Making it Happen – Improving the Basic Skills of the Workforce* (including video, 25 minutes), Basic Skills Agency, London

BSA (1995) *A Study of Effectiveness – Basic Skills at Work Programmes*, Basic Skills Agency: London

BSA (1998) *Basic Skills Quality Mark for Post-16 programmes*, Basic Skills Agency, London

BSA (2001) (a) *The Adult Numeracy Core Curriculum* and *The Adult Literacy Core Curriculum*, Basic Skills Agency, London

BSA (2001) (b) *Mapping Literacy and Numeracy Standards to National Occupational Standards* series of booklets, Basic Skills Agency, London

BSI Quality Assurance (1994) *What is BS EN ISO 9000?*, BSI Quality Assurance, Milton Keynes

Carnevale, AP, Gainer, LJ and Meltzer, AS (1990) *Workplace Basics. The Skills Employers Want* American Society for Training and Development, US Dept. of Labor, Washington DC

Darville, R. (1992) *The Economic Push for Literacy: Expansive or Restrictive?*, UNESCO, New York

DfEE (2001) *Skills for Life: the National Strategy for Improving Adult Literacy and Numeracy Skills*, DfEE, London

Department of Trade and Industry (a) *Quality Circles: an Executive Guide* Managing in the 90s Series, DTI, London, nd

Department of Trade and Industry (b) *The Quality Gurus – What Can They Do for Your Company?* Managing in the 90s series, DTI, London, nd

Department of Trade and Industry (c) *Total Quality Management and Effective Leadership: a Strategic Overview.* Managing in the 90s series, DTI, London, nd

Department of Trade and Industry (d) *Statistical Process Control – an Introduction to Quash Improvement.* Managing in the 90s series, DTI, London, nd

Forrester, K, Payne, J and Ward, K (1995) *Workplace Learning*, Avebury Ashgate Publishing Ltd, Aldershot

Frank, F and Hamilton, M (1993) *Not Just a Number: The Role of Basic Skills Programmes in the Changing Workplace*, CSET, Lancaster University, Lancaster

Frank, F (2001) Session V: "Workplace Basic Skills: a key part of the Government Lifelong Learning Agenda" in Holland, C (ed) *Diploma in Adult Basic Education: Workplace Module Participant Support Pack 2*, CSET Lancaster University, Lancaster

Helsby, G (2000), *A Cinderella Service: the View from the Coach – Evaluation of the Workplace Basic Skills Training Network Professional Development Programme*, GH Evaluations, Kendal

Holland, C, Frank, F and Cooke, T (1998) *Literacy and the New Work Order – An International Literature Review*, NIACE, Leicester

ISO (2001) *ISO 9000* http://beta.iso.ch/iso/en/iso9000-14000/iso9000/iso9000index.html

Jackson, N. (2000) "Writing Up People at Work: Investigations of Workplace Literacy" in Working Knowledge: Productive Learning at Work, Conference Proceedings 10–13 December, University of Technology, Sydney, New South Wales, Australia: Research in Adult and Vocational Learning, Faculty of Education, University of Technology, Sydney

Lankshear, C (1994) "Self Direction and Empowerment: Critical Language Awareness and the 'New Work Order'" in O'Connor, P (ed) *Thinking Work Volume I*, ALBSAC, Leichhardt, NSW

McGivney, V (1990) *Education's for Other People: Access to Education for Non-participant Adults. A Research Report*, NIACE, Leicester

McGivney, V (1994) *Wasted Potential: Training and Career Progression for Part-Time and Temporary Workers*, NIACE, Leicester

Mace, J and Yarnit, M (1987) (Eds) *Time Off To Learn: Paid Educational Leave and Low Paid Workers*, Methuen, London

NACETT (1998)
http://www.open.gov.uk/dfee/nacte/traintar.htm

O'Connor, P (1 994) (ed) *Thinking Work Volume I*, ALBSAC, Leichhardt, NSW

O'Connor, P (1995) *Making it Happen: Developing Effective Workplace Basic Skills Programs*, ALBSAC, Leichhardt, NSW

Park, A (1994) *Individual Commitment to Learning: Individuals' Attitudes*, Employment Department, Sheffield

QCA (2001) *National Standards for Adult Literacy and Numeracy*, Qualifications and Curriculum Authority.

Rees, L (1990) *Setting Up Workplace Basic Skills Training – Guidelines for practitioners*, Workbase Training ALBSU (now BSA), London

Taylor, M (ed) (1997) *Workplace Education: The Changing Landscape*, Culture Concepts, Ontario

Taylor, M, Lewe, G and Draper, J (eds) (1991) *Basic Skills for the Workplace*, Culture Concepts Inc, Toronto, Ontario

TUC (1998) *Learning in the Workplace* ref: ET045, TUC Learning Services, Liverpool

TUC (1999) *Employee Development Schemes: Case Studies of Union Involvement* ref: E1057 TUC Learning Services, Liverpool

TUC (1999) *Learning with the Unions* ref: ET055, TUC Learning Services, Liverpool

TUC (2000) *Better Basic Skills: A handbook for union representatives*, Trades Union Congress in partnership with CTAD and the Basic Skills Agency, TUC Learning Services, Liverpool

Wilkinson, S (1994) *Quality and Workplace Education: A Guide for Practitioners*, Scottish Community Education Council, Edinburgh

Useful addresses

Adult Basic Skills Strategy Unit
DfES: Department for Education and Skills
Caxton House
Tothill Street
Westminster
London
SW1H 9NF
Email: andrew.graham@dfes.gsi.gov.uk
Website: www.dfes.gov.uk/readwriteplus/
and www.lifelonglearning.dfes.gov.uk
Includes a directory of Lifelong Learning Partnerships

Adult Learning Inspectorate
101 Lockhurst Lane
Coventry
CV6 5SF
Tel: 0870 240 7744
Fax: 0870 242 1444
Email: enquiries@ali.gov.uk
Website: www.ali.gov.uk

Adult Literacy and Numeracy in Scotland
The Adult Literacy National Training Project
Apex House
99 Haymarket Terrace
Edinburgh
EH12 5HD
Tel: 0131 313 6230
Email: Karen.geekie@scotent.co.uk

Avanti Books
8 Parsons Green
Boulton Road
Pin Green Industrial Estate
Stevenage
SG1 4QG
Tel: 01438 745877
Fax: 01438 741131
Email: avantihil@aol.com
Website: www.avantibooks.com/cgi-bin/avantibooks.storefront

BSA (The Basic Skills Agency)
7th Floor
Commonwealth House
1-19 New Oxford Street
London WC1A 1NU
Tel: 020 7405 4017
Fax: 020 7440 6626
Email: enquiries@basic-skills.co.uk
Website: www.basic-skills.co.uk

Basic Skills Agency Publications – Orderline
Admail 524
London
WC1A 1BR, UK
Tel: 0870 600 2400
Fax: 0870 600 2401
Email: basicskills@twoten.press.net

Basic Skills Unit, Northern Ireland
EGSA
4th Floor
40 Linenhall Street
Belfast
Northern Ireland
BT2 8BA
Tel: 028 9024 4274
Email: bsu@egsa.org.uk
Website: www.basic-skills-ni.com/

Campaign for Learning
19 Buckingham Street
London
WC2N 6EF
Tel: 020 7930 1111
Fax: 020 7930 1551
Email: tgreany@cflearning.org.uk
Website: www.campaign-for-learning.org.uk

CBI: Confederation of British Industry
Centre Point
103 New Oxford Street
London
WC1A 1DU
Tel: 020 7395 8247
Fax: 020 7240 1578
Website: www.cbi.org.uk

EMPNTO: The Employment NTO
Kimberley House
47 Vaughan Way
Leicester
LE1 4SG
Tel: 0116 251 7979
Fax: 0116 251 1464
e-mail: info@empnto.co.uk
website: www.empnto.co.uk/

FENTO: Further Education National Training Organisation
5th Floor
103 New Oxford St
London
WC1A 1DD
Tel: 020 7827 4666
Email: info@fento.org
Website: www.fento.co.uk

IiP: Investors In People UK
7-10 Chandos Street
London
W1M 9DE
Tel: 020 7467 1900
Fax: 020 7636 2386
Email: information@iipuk.co.uk
Website: www.iipuk.co.uk

LSC: Learning and Skills Council
Cheylesmore House
Quinton Road
Coventry
CV1 2WT
Tel: 0845 019 4170
Fax: 024 7686 3100
Email: info@lsc.gov.uk
Website: www.lsc.gov.uk
(provides links to all Local Learning and Skills Councils in England)

Learning and Skills Development Agency
Citadel Place
Tinworth Street
London SE11 5EH
Tel: 020 7840 5400
Fax: 020 7840 5401
Email: enquiries@lsda.org.uk
Website: www.lsda.org. uk

London Language and Literacy Unit (LLLU)
South Bank University
103 Borough Road
London
SE1 0AA
Tel: 020 7815 6290
Fax: 020 7815 6296
email: LLLU@sbu.ac.uk
website: www.sbu.ac.uk/caxton/LLLU/

NATECLA
National Association for Teaching English and Other
   Community Languages to Adults
Emilia Prodanova
Administrator
NATECLA National Centre
South Birmingham College
99-103 Clifton Road
Birmingham
B12 8SR
Tel: 0121 688 8121
Fax: 0121 449 9070
Website: www.natecla.org.uk/

National Literacy Trust
Swire House
59 Buckingham Gate
London
SW1E 6AJ
Tel: 020 7828 2435
Fax: 020 7931 9986
Email: contact@literacytrust.org.uk
Website: www.literacytrust.org.uk/

NIACE
21 De Montfort Street
Leicester
LE1 7GE
Tel: 0116 204 4200/1
Fax: 0116 285 4514
Email: niace@niace.org.uk
Website: www.niace.org.uk

NTO National Council Head Office
10 Meadow Court
Amos Road
Sheffield
S9 1BX
Tel: 0114 2619926
Fax: 0114 261 8103
Email: info@nto-nc.org
Website: www.nto-nc.org/
Includes links to Regional Development Agencies as well as NTO National Council regional managers and to all the National Training Organisations.

OCNW: Open College of the North West
Storey Institute
Meeting House Lane
Lancaster
LA1 1TH
Tel: 01524 845046
Fax: 01524 388467
Email: ocnw@lancaster.ac.uk
Website: www.ocnw.com

PAULO: The National Training Organisation (NTO) for community-based learning and development
Springfield House
Springfield Road
Grantham
NG31 7BG
Tel: 01476 514628
Fax: 01476 514629
Website: www.paulo.org.uk

QCA: Qualifications and Curriculum Authority
29 Bolton Street
London
W1Y 7PD
Tel: 020 7509 5555
Fax: 020 7509 6666
Website: www.qca.org.uk

RaPAL (Research and Practice in Adult Literacy)
Wendy Moss
Membership Secretary
The City Lit Training Unit
The City Lit
Stukeley Street
London
WC2B 5LJ
Website: www.literacy.lancs.ac.uk/rapal/rapal.htm

Skills and Enterprise Network
FREEPOST 396
London
SW1P 3DE
Tel: 01564 796603
Fax: 01564 796609
Email: dfes@prolog.uk.com
Website: www.dfee.gov.uk/skillnet/

Social Exclusion Unit
Cabinet Office
35 Great Smith St
London
SW1P 3BQ
Tel: 020 7276 2055
Fax: 020 7276 2056
Email: alan.parsons@cabinet-office.x.gsi.gov.uk
Website: www.cabinet-office.gov.uk/seu/

TUC: Trades Union Congress
TUC Learning Services
Suite 506-510
The Cotton Exchange
Old Hall Street
Liverpool
L3 9UD
Tel: 0151 236 7678
Fax: 0151 236 2331
Website: www.tuc.org.uk/

UfI/Learndirect
The Innovation Centre
217 Portobello Street
Sheffield
S1 4DP
Tel: 0114 224 2999
Fax: 0114 270 0034
Email: enquiries@ufi.cwc.com
Website: www.ufiltd.co.uk

WEA: Workers' Educational Association
Temple House
17 Victoria Park Square
London
E2 9PB
Tel: 020 8983 1515
Fax: 020 8983 4840
Email: info@wea.org.uk
Website: www.wea.org.uk

Workbase Training
Finchley House Business Centre
707 High Road
Finchley
London
N12 0BT
Tel: 020 8492 0330
Fax: 020 8492 0405
Website: www.workbase.org.uk

Workplace Basic Skills Network
CSET
Lancaster University
Lancaster
LA1 4YL
Tel: 01524 583405
Fax: 01524 844788
Email: wbs.net@lancaster.ac.uk
Website: www.lancaster.ac.uk/wbsnet
Contains links to all these agencies and more

Appendix

The Workplace Basic Skills Network is a national membership organisation based at Lancaster University, within CSET, the Centre for the Study of Education and Training in the Education Research Department. The Network builds professional capacity in workplace basic skills provision, through continuing professional development, networking and other support services including:

- Seminars and workshops
- A regular Bulletin
- Consultancy and support for providers, including the management of the 'Building Basic Skills in the Workplace' DfES-funded initiative.
- Research
- National and international links and partnership projects
- Support for regional networks.

Workplace Basic Skills Network progression pathways map[1]

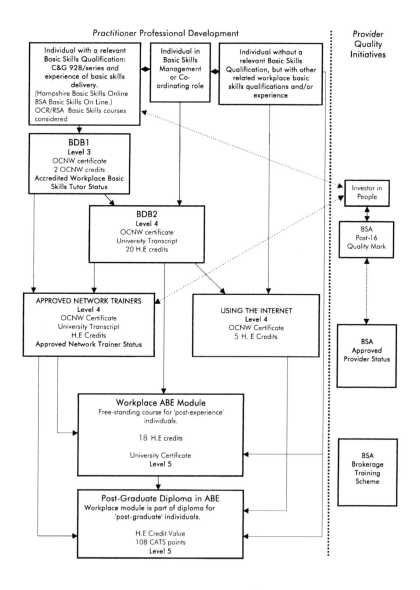

Practitioner Professional Development

Individual with a relevant Basic Skills Qualification: C&G 928/series and experience of basic skills delivery. (Hampshire Basic Skills Online BSA Basic Skills On Line.) OCR/RSA Basic Skills courses considered

Individual in Basic Skills Management or Co-ordinating role

Individual without a relevant Basic Skills Qualification, but with other related workplace basic skills qualifications and/or experience

Provider Quality Initiatives

BDB1
Level 3
OCNW certificate
2 OCNW credits
Accredited Workplace Basic Skills Tutor Status

BDB2
Level 4
OCNW certificate
University Transcript
20 H.E credits

APPROVED NETWORK TRAINERS
Level 4
OCNW Certificate
University Transcript
H.E Credits
Approved Network Trainer Status

USING THE INTERNET
Level 4
OCNW Certificate
5 H. E Credits

Workplace ABE Module
Free-standing course for 'post-experience' individuals.

18 H.E credits

University Certificate
Level 5

Post-Graduate Diploma in ABE
Workplace module is part of diploma for 'post-graduate' individuals.

H.E Credit Value
108 CATS points
Level 5

Investor in People

BSA
Post-16
Quality Mark

BSA
Approved
Provider Status

BSA
Brokerage
Training
Scheme

---

[1] Chisholm Caunt 2000

Diagram illustrating the relationship between new basic skills initiatives[2]

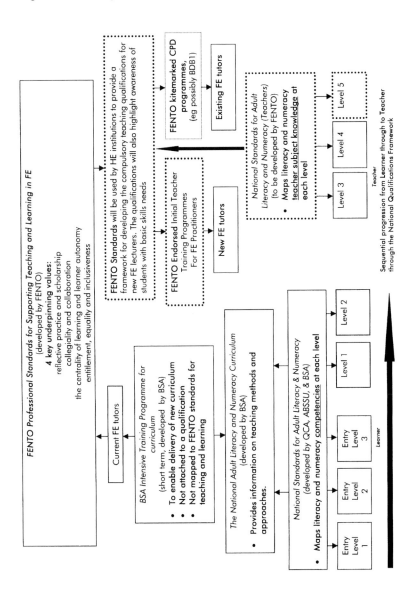

[2] Chisholm Caunt and Holland 2001

Other books from NIACE

Literacy and the new work order
an international literature review

edited by Chris Holland with Tony Cooke and Fiona Frank

ISBN 1 86201 018 8
April 1998, 148pp
£10.00

In the last two decades, lobbyists and interest groups of the New Right have presented literacy as an economic imperative, by an inverse process of blaming lack of economic competitiveness on those who lack skills needed for the New Work Order. Policy reponse in advanced capitalist countries has been to promote lifelong learning in the form of skills for work. This book offers the reader much more than an annotated review. Written by an experienced practitioner and consultant in workplace literacy, the review discusses theories in a way which makes them accessible and connected to practice.

Texts are included which critique or support the rhetoric of the New Work Order, and an analysis is provided according to major themes: Crisis and Competitiveness, High Performance Workplaces and The Learning Organisation. These themes and the issues they present are explored in five advanced capitalist nations: Britain, Canada, the United States, Australia and New Zealand. The implications of the debate for literacy practice in the workplace are examined throughout. Finally, it includes a section of annotations and a bibliography.

The book can be used as both an annotated reference for workplace literacy texts and as a discussion of themes and issues which need to be further explored. Aimed primarily at workplace literacy education organisers and practitioners, it is of interest to any researcher, adult educator, workplace trainer and trade unionist wanting to learn about organisational change and the implications for adult literacy.

Learning organisations
What they are and how to become one

Alan Clarke

ISBN 1 86201 116 8
September 2001, 56pp
£7.95

This book identifies the need, in today's rapidly-developing business world, for organisations to be ready to adapt to change in order to survive and prosper. To do so entails the need to be able to learn, by recognising the value of individual, team and organisational learning. By encouraging individuals and teams to accept responsibility and authority for their actions, and by encouraging risk-taking, businesses are more likely to reap rewards of innovation, creativity and improved employee motivation and performance.

Having identified some key characteristics, the book goes on to suggest what organisations can do to become learning organisations, with a series of exercises and discussion points to be used in the workplace. The role of senior mangement is shown to be vital in giving a clear signal about how learning is seen to be integral to business objectives.

There is a list of useful contacts, and an excellent review of literature on the subject of the learning organisation.

This book will be beneficial to all businesses, whether in manufacturing or services, who wish to maximise the potential of their employees.

Develop the worker
Develop the business
A guide for smaller businesses
Veronica McGivney

ISBN 1 86201 031 5
October 1997, 108pp
£25.00

The majority of British workers are employed in small and medium-sized enterprises. The smaller the firm, the fewer the opportunities for staff training and development. However, many do overcome the obstacles and are able to develop their staff, with considerable benefits both for the businesses and the individuals concerned.

This guide is based on recent research and on the first-hand testimony of small business owners, managers and employees, as well as training providers. Aimed at owners or managers of small businesses, this guide is designed to be a basic practical manual for those who want to initiate or improve staff training and development activities but are unsure of how to do it.

Illustrated by case study material, the guide also includes examples of a range of approaches and strategies which can be used to overcome obstacles faced by small and medium-sized enterprises. There are facts and figures about SMEs, flexible working and employer-provided training; a look at specific constraints and difficulties; the business case for training; ideas on motivating employees to participate in training; and an examination of skill needs.

Earning and learning – Developing the adult workforce
Alastair Thomson

ISBN 1 86201 120 6
March 2002, Approx 60pp
£8.95

This publication examines how the workplace and employment relationship can contribute to a society where recurrent access to education and training is more common and equitably distributed. It explores ways of analysing central issues and problems; approaches in balancing public and private resource contributions; and methods and initiatives which might deliver the desired objectives.